BOOKS: FROM PAPYRUS
TO PAPERBACK

The first part of this book tells the fascinating story of books from their earliest beginnings nearly six thousand years ago: clay tablets, papyrus scrolls, codices, parchment and vellum manuscripts, the coming of paper to Europe, and the invention and development of printing.

The second part, written largely from the authors' personal experience, surveys the book world in Britain today, including authorship, publishing, book production, bookshops and libraries. It offers practical help to all those who would like to enjoy and use books more fully.

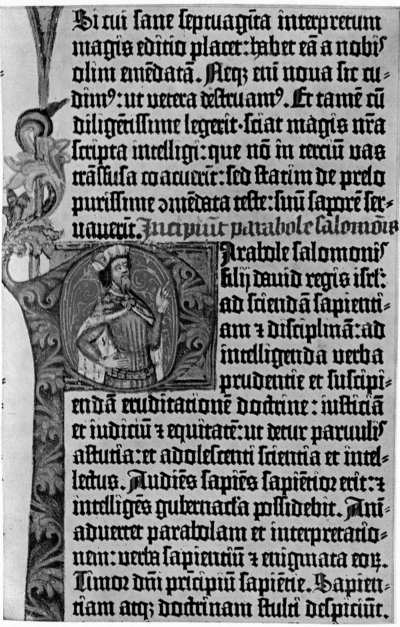

Si cui sane septuagita interpretum magis editio placet: habet eā a nobis olim emēdatā. Aeq; eni noua sic cudim⁹: ut vetera destruam⁹. Et tamē tū diligētissime legerit·sciat magis nra scripta intelligi: que nō in tertiū vas trāsfusa coacuerit: sed statim de prelo purissime ēmēdata teste: suū saporē seruauerit. Incipiūt parabole salomōis

Ratole salomonis filij dauid regis isrl: ad sciendā sapientiam & disciplinā: ad intelligenda verba prudentie et suscipiendā eruditacōne doctrine: iusticiā et iudiciū & equitatē: ut detur paruulis astucia: et adolescenti scientia et intellectus. Audiēs sapiēs sapiētior erit: & intelligēs gubernacla possidebit. Aniaduertet parabolam et interpretacōnem: verba sapientiū & enigmata eoᷓ. Timor dñi pricipiū sapiētie. Sapientiam atq; doctrinam stulti despiciūt.

The beginning of the Book of Proverbs in the famous Gutenberg Bible, the first book ever printed from movable type. King Solomon appears in the illuminated initial, which was painted by hand. The Bible was printed by Johannes Gutenberg at Mainz, Germany in 1452–5

BOOKS: FROM
PAPYRUS TO PAPERBACK

---

by Esther S. Harley, B.A., A.L.A.
and John Hampden, M.A.

ROY PUBLISHERS, INC. NEW YORK

Printed in Great Britain

ACKNOWLEDGEMENTS

The authors and publisher gratefully acknowledge permission from the following to reproduce illustrations. Pages 16, 25, 39 and 40, the Trustees of the British Museum; 29, 55 and 78, the Bodleian Library, Oxford; 15 and 17 (top), Mr David Diringer and Messrs Thames & Hudson Ltd; 23 and 65 (top), Mr Sean Jennett and Messrs Faber & Faber Ltd; 33, 36 and 43, St Bride's Printing Library; 65 (bottom), the Monotype Corporation Ltd; 66 (top), Mr Hugh Williamson and the Oxford University Press. Illustrations on pages 69–70 and 74 are based on Harold Curwen's Puffin Picture book on *Printing* with the publisher's permission. The publishers' devices on pages 58–9 were kindly supplied by Cambridge University Press, Oxford University Press, Penguin Books Ltd, André Deutsch Ltd, George Allen & Unwin Ltd, J. M. Dent & Sons Ltd, Rupert Hart Davis, Longmans, Green and The Folio Society Ltd. The Folio Society device was engraved on wood by Reynolds Stone in 1947.

The Trustees of the British Museum generously lent the blocks for the frontispiece.

CONTENTS

I. THE PAST

The Beginnings   *page* 7
Writing on Clay   8
Egyptian Scrolls   11
Books in Ancient Greece and Rome 16
The Dead Sea Scrolls   22
The Wider World   24
Medieval Splendour   26
Paper   32
The Invention of Printing   34
The Book Trade Develops   41
Technical Progress   45
A Wider Reading Public   48
The Art of the Book   50

II. THE PRESENT

A Book is Written   *page* 53
Few are Chosen   57
Designing Books   59
Making Books   64
Marketing Books   76
The Bookseller's Role   80
Libraries for All   82
The Paperback Revolution   86
How Books can Help You   88

Acknowledgements and Book
  List   92
Index   94

I. THE PAST

The Beginnings

FOR MANY THOUSANDS of years men lived with no approach to writing, apart from pictures which they scratched on wood or bone or painted on the walls of caves. In those distant prehistoric times songs and stories and messages were simply passed on by word of mouth. But as men began to live in larger, settled communities, and life became more complicated, they felt the need for written records. Bills, receipts, accounts and so forth came first. Civilisation cannot exist without book-keeping. Records of Government business are also very ancient, and other records followed. Letters had to be sent to people at a distance, treaties had to be made between kings and contracts between merchants, and legal systems had to be established. Scientific knowledge began to accumulate, and works of literature became longer and more numerous.

All these things and many others needed to be written down as civilisation developed, so that they could be clearly understood, accurately remembered, and passed from one person or place to another without being distorted as oral messages so often are. The ancient Egyptians, realising the tremendous importance of writing, called it "the speech of the gods", and for centuries the few people who could read and write were regarded with awe—or suspicion.

It took thousands of years, however, for the first attempts to develop into the kind of alphabetic writing which most of the world uses today, and centuries longer for something like the book, as we know it, to be invented.

Naturally enough, writing began with pictures of people and things, and a series of drawings could, rather clumsily, tell a story or convey an idea. A tablet with a drawing of three sheep could be given as a receipt for three sheep, but suppose there were three thousand sheep? Such *pictographs*, as they are now called, are still used today by some primitive peoples in Africa and South America. The oldest pictographs known are on a limestone tablet which was found at Kish on the River Euphrates and has been dated at about 3500 B.C.

Then pictures of things were used to express actions and ideas. A drawing of a man's foot could mean "to walk", or "a journey"; a drawing of the sun could

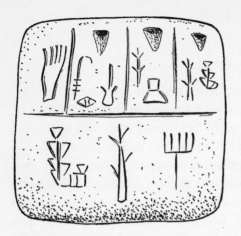

The picture-writing (pictographs) scratched on this Sumerian limestone tablet about 3500 B.C. or earlier may be the oldest kind of writing in the world. The signs include numbers, an implement for threshing corn, and a hand

stand for "day" or "heat". Such *ideographs*, drawings representing ideas, carried writing a stage further, and they are still used by the Chinese today, although Chinese writing began about 1500 B.C., but they had very serious drawbacks. Although the pictures were simplified, it was slow and tedious to draw a large number of them. They had no relation to the sounds of spoken words. And hundreds or even thousands of different signs had to be used, so that only a few highly trained people, usually the priests, could learn to write and read. The next stage was *syllabic* writing, which is used by the Japanese today, and some other peoples, in which signs represented the sounds of separate syllables. This was developed by the Persians and others. At last, after centuries of experiment, came *alphabetic* writing, which needed only a few signs, about thirty *letters*, for writing down any word or sound in the spoken language. It is used to day in most modern languages. Some of them, such as Greek, Russian, Arabic, Urdu, Hindi and Indonesian, use alphabets different from the Roman alphabet in which this book is printed and which is now used by all West European languages and some others. But all true alphabets follow the same method; they use a small number of signs, more or less phonetic, which can be put together in groups to represent all the sounds and words in the language. The alphabet has made it possible for almost anyone to learn to read and write, and it is one of the most important of all human inventions.

Writing on Clay

It was in the Middle East that the first civilisations seem to have begun, round about 4000 B.C., in the valleys of the Tigris and Euphrates (Mesopotamia), in the

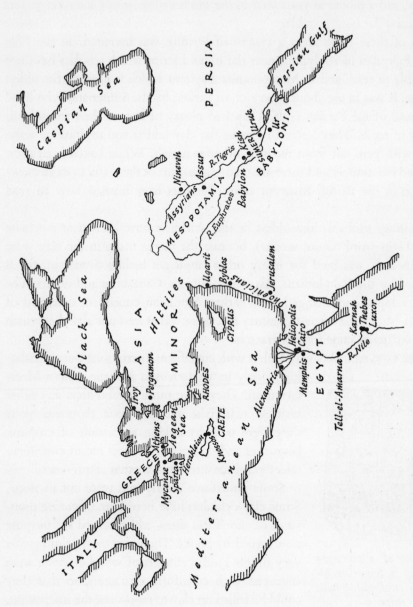

This map shows many of the most important centres of civilisation in the ancient world, including the rivers Tigris, Euphrates and Nile. The river Indus, in what is now West Pakistan and India, is to the right of the map. The Minoans in Crete later used several scripts, and one of these, known as Linear B, has recently been deciphered

Nile valley, and a thousand years later in the Indus valley, where the river waters made extensive farming possible.

In each of these three areas a system of writing was invented: in the Nile valley the Egyptian hieroglyphic, near the Indus a script which scholars have not yet been able to read, and in Mesopotamia a system which is possibly the oldest of the three. It was in use about 3500 B.C., or earlier, by the Sumerians, who lived near the head of the Persian Gulf. They had plenty of clay in their marshlands and plenty of reeds. They learned to make flat clay tablets and to draw or write on them with pens cut from reeds or other materials. When baked hard these tablets lasted indefinitely and there are many thousands of them still in existence—over 25,000 in the British Museum alone. Scholars have learned how to read them.

This writing, probably the oldest in the world, is now known as *cuneiform* (from the Latin word *cuneus*, wedge), because the marks made in the clay were wedge-shaped. It was used for many other languages besides Sumerian, for it was adopted by the Babylonians, Assyrians, Hittites, Canaanites and others. The writing developed and changed. The earliest Sumerian cuneiform consisted of pictographs, but by the fifteenth century B.C. there was at least one alphabet which was being written in cuneiform characters.

By about 1500 B.C., also, clay tablets with cuneiform inscriptions were circulating widely in western Asia and the eastern Mediterranean. They were more durable than any other writing materials, and for four thousand years they were used by a long succession of empires, languages and cultures. The most recent cuneiform tablet yet discovered was written about 6 B.C.

A clay tablet of about 2900 B.C. bearing a Sumerian inscription in semi-pictographic script

Some cuneiform inscriptions were cut in stone. Some clay cylinders have been found, bearing thousands of cuneiform signs, which served the purpose now served by books. There was even printing of a very simple kind; cylinders of wood or stone were engraved with cuneiform characters, so that they could be rolled on clay to reproduce the inscription.

Clay tablets can barely be called books. The great collections of them which have been found in excavating some of the buried cities of the Middle East can barely be called libraries. But they obviously served the same purpose. A good many consisted mainly or entirely of commercial and government "documents", but there are exceptions and one of these, at least, deserves special mention—the great "library" at Nineveh, the ancient capital of Assyria, which was discovered by the British archaeologist, Sir Austen Henry Layard, in 1853.

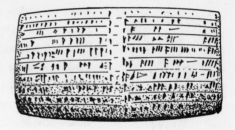

A clay tablet of the sixth century B.C. with a cuneiform inscription

The last ruler of the powerful Assyrian Empire was Ashur-bani-pal, (or Asser-bani-pal), who was a famous general and much more. He formed a great "library" of clay tablets, setting scholars to collect literary, historical, religious and scientific works, and to make good translations and editions of them. One of these was a translation from the Sumerian language of the group of poems about Gilgamesh, a legendary hero, who was well known in the ancient world. These poems included the Babylonian account of the Deluge—"Noah's Flood", which is also described in the Bible: *Genesis*, chapters 6 to 9. There is a direct link between these clay tablets and the modern paperback; in 1960 *The Epic of Gilgamesh*, an English version, with an introduction by N. K. Sanders, was published in the Penguin Classics. These poems may well have been composed five thousand years ago, long before the *Iliad* and the *Odyssey*, and they make good reading still.

Egyptian Scrolls

The Nile has long been one of the most famous rivers in the world, and rightly so, for its waters nourished the splendid civilisations of ancient Egypt for some four thousand years B.C. as they still fertilise the parched lands of Egypt today. So it was very appropriate that a water plant, which grew profusely along the shores of the Upper Nile and in its delta should have proved the most useful of all the plants growing in ancient Egypt. This was the papyrus, a reed with a bare

Papyrus plants which grew along the banks of the river Nile. The tallest were fifteen or sixteen feet high. The writing material was made from the pith of these plants

stem as much as sixteen feet in height, crowned by a head of feathery foliage which might be three feet across. The foliage made garlands for the altars of the Egyptians' gods. (They were a very religious people.) The wood of the roots was carved into various utensils, or served as fuel. The stems were used to make many things, from boats and sandals to ropes and mats. (The little floating cradle in which the baby Moses was found by Pharaoh's daughter was most probably woven of papyrus.) Most important of all, the pith was made into a writing material, probably the first thing of its kind in history, which came to be used all over the Mediterranean world and was known as *papyrus*. (Our word *paper* is derived from it, although the two materials are quite different.)

The pith of the plant was cut into short pieces and these were split with a sharp knife into very thin strips as broad as possible. These were laid close together vertically on a board and were covered with a second layer placed horizontally. The strips were then moistened with glue, pressed under weights or in a press, and dried in the sun. After the surface had been smoothed with pumice stone and a piece of ivory or a shell, it was coated with a thin paste of fine flour, water and vinegar, and finally dried and pressed again.

There were different qualities of papyrus, the best being made from the centre of the pith. The sheets were often about nine inches wide, but could vary from four or five inches to twelve or even more. The height of the page also varied, being anything up to nineteen inches.

Sheets were often used singly, for letters or bills, for example. Often, however, they were glued or sewn edge to edge to make long strips which were rolled up. Egyptian *papyri* could be fifty feet long, or a hundred. The longest known, the "Harris Papyrus" in the British Museum, a chronicle of the reign of Rameses II, is 133 feet long.

A round stick might be fastened along one end or both, so that the papyrus could be rolled more easily. Sometimes the scrolls were put into jars. When the scrolls were laid on shelves in libraries a label was fastened to the end of each so that it could be identified.

Papyrus was the best and most widely used writing material in the ancient world. It had one great drawback—it perished easily. In Egypt the remarkably dry hot climate preserved it along with many other ancient remains; our museums today contain thousands of papyri in good condition which have been found in Egypt. In other countries, however, papyrus soon discoloured and fell to pieces, so clay tablets, or sheets of leather or metal, had to be used for writing which was to be kept permanently. But for general use papyrus was unequalled. It was thin, flexible, light in weight, smooth to write on. It was made almost entirely in Egypt, but there was plenty of it and it was freely exported.

The Egyptians invented papyrus some time before 3500 B.C. and from early times Egyptian civilisation was based on reading and writing, beginning with the famous script which the Greeks later named *hieroglyphics*, "sacred carved letters", because it was so much used for religious inscriptions. When skilfully carved on stone or written with coloured inks on the best papyrus by an expert scribe, hieroglyphics are one of the most beautiful scripts ever invented. Moreover, many Egyptian books were beautifully illustrated.

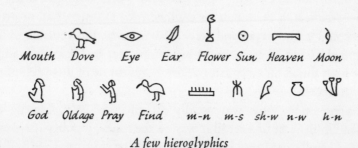

A few hieroglyphics

Hieroglyphics began as pictographs. They developed into ideographs, each sign representing a word or an idea, and signs for sounds were used with them from early times. In fact, hieroglyphics nearly developed into an alphabetic script —but apparently not quite.

They had to be written or painted slowly, however, so the Egyptians soon invented the *hieratic* script, or "priest's writing", which was quicker, and by the seventh century B.C. a still simpler script, the *demotic*, or "people's writing" which had been evolved from the hieratic. Hieroglyphics were written in any direction, often vertically; hieratic and demotic were written from right to left. All three ways of writing the Egyptian language were used together so long as the kingdoms of the Pharaohs lasted.

Afterwards the art of reading the scripts was lost, and "hieroglyphics" came to be used loosely for any kind of writing which was unreadable, but from the seventeenth century A.D., European scholars tried to decipher them—one of the most exciting and difficult pieces of detective work ever undertaken. The most important clues were found on the famous Rosetta Stone, a slab of black basalt now in the British Museum, which was dug up in Egypt in 1799. It commemorates the coronation of Ptolemy V in 196 B.C., and the inscription is in Egyptian and Greek, the Egyptian being given twice, in hieroglyphic and demotic, the Greek in Greek letters. As the ability to read Greek had never been lost, this stone was invaluable, and when the French scholar Champollion completed the solution of the mystery in 1824 the key to a lost civilisation was found.

Books and writing were as essential to education in ancient Egypt as they are in Britain today, and the young Egyptian who was to become a priest or a civil servant, an architect, a doctor or an engineer, for example, had to go to school so that he could learn to read and write. Papyrus was too valuable to be wasted, so he practised first of all on pieces of broken pottery and flat stones and many of these have been found on Egyptian rubbish heaps, some of them full of the oddest schoolboy mistakes.

The writing on papyrus was usually on one side only, because it showed through, and in the case of a scroll it was on the inside, in fairly narrow columns. The scribe generally used two brush-pens, made of reeds, and red and black ink. The red was used to mark the beginning of a new chapter or paragraph, and this was continued in ancient Greece and Rome and in medieval Europe. In Christian service books the instructions to the priest and congregation were written, and later printed, in red, to distinguish them from the words to be spoken, and were therefore called *rubrics* (from the Latin *ruber*, red). They are still given this name in

Christian prayer books today—a direct link with the Egyptian manuscripts of three thousand years B.C.

The Egyptian scrolls, the long or short rolls of papyrus, which had to be unrolled with one hand and rolled up with the other when they were being read, were not nearly so convenient as our books, and since they took a good deal of space they were more troublesome to store, but they served their purpose well enough. Every copy of every book had to be written slowly by hand, of course, but there is no doubt that many thousands were produced. Today there are hundreds in museums. Religious books are in the majority, because all the professional scribes seem to have been priests, but there are also collections of poems or stories or medical prescriptions, scientific works and so on.

Wooden palettes used by Egyptian scribes. The two circles in the left-hand palette were used for the two inks, red and black. The brush-pens were made from reeds.

Some kind of organised publishing and bookselling may have begun, but apparently no records of it have been found. There may be truth in the old joke that the first booksellers were undertakers, for the men who organised Egyptian funerals (often very elaborate and expensive) sold copies of the most famous, most often reproduced, of all Egyptian books: *The Book of the Dead*.

The Egyptians believed that after death everyone came up for judgment by the gods and had to answer a series of questions. Those who failed in the test were devoured by a monster: those who passed lived happily in the kingdom of the great god Osiris.

A full account of this trial, with all the questions and answers, was written in *The Book of the Dead*, the chief mourners had copies and a copy was put in the

A short part of the Book of the Dead

tomb for the guidance of the dead person in the next world. *The Book of the Dead* was copied, in one form or another, for more than three thousand years, until the second century A.D. Naturally it varied a great deal from age to age, but the finest copies, which contain many pictures, are masterpieces of book production.

Books in Ancient Greece and Rome

No one knows exactly when or where the first true alphabetic writing appeared, or whether it was invented by a great individual genius or was developed from earlier scripts. These things may be discovered one day. It is known, however, from inscriptions found in Syria that a completely alphabetic script was being used there by the fifteenth or sixteenth century B.C. A number of alphabets developed from this, the most important to us being that used by the Phoenicians,

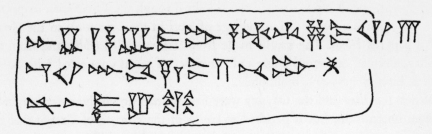

The oldest complete ABC which is known, a cuneiform alphabet of thirty-two letters. This is one of hundreds of clay tablets, dating from the fifteenth and fourteenth centuries B.C., which were found in 1929 at Ugarit on the Syrian coast

an adventurous seafaring people who lived along the Syrian coast and who not only sailed all over the Mediterranean, founding colonies at Carthage and in Malta, Sicily and other places, but reached Britain and sailed all round Africa.

The Phoenician alphabet, which was very like the Hebrew alphabet, consisted of twenty-two letters very easy to write—a vast improvement on those ideographic scripts which needed hundreds or thousands of characters. At some time, probably between 1000 and 700 B.C., the Greeks adopted it and made alphabets which became the classical Greek alphabet of twenty-four letters. They adopted the names of the letters too. The Phoenicians called their first letter *alph* and their second *beth*; the Greeks called theirs *alpha* and *beta*, from which we get out own word *alphabet*.

The Greeks improved their letters, as the drawing shows, and although at first they wrote from right to left, as most other peoples had done, after the fifth century B.C. they wrote from left to right—a great advantage, for right-handed people at least, and one of the many things for which we are indebted to them.

From the Phoenicians they obtained not only the best kind of writing, but the best material to write on—papyrus. This came

Phoenician	Greek	Roman
⟨	A	A
9	B	B
⟩	‹	C
⟨	△	D
⟩	E	E

This shows in simplified form the development of some of our letters. The earlier Greek letters were more like the Phoenician

from Egypt, and it often reached the Greeks through the Phoenician seaport of Byblos (which is now the fishing village of Jebal in the Lebanon), so the Greeks called papyrus *biblos*. The scrolls made from it they called *biblia*, and from this we have derived our word Bible and a number of terms connected with books, such as bibliography and bibliophile.

When the *Iliad* and the *Odyssey* were first written down they were probably written on papyrus, but it perished so easily in the climate of Greece that our knowledge of Greek literature—one of the greatest the world has ever known—comes largely from later copies on papyrus found in Egypt and still later copies on parchment found in other countries. A great deal of Greek literature disappeared completely.

Greek scrolls were smaller than Egyptian. A pocket volume of poems might be only five inches high and a few feet long, but ten inches was a commoner height for other books, and the average length was probably twenty to thirty feet. A work which now goes into one small volume might need a dozen heavy scrolls, and finding a particular passage in one of them must have been far more tedious than finding it in a printed book. The papyrus had to be rolled up at the left and unrolled at the right, until the page was found.

Reading, too, was more difficult becausetherewerenospacesbetweenwords and no punctuation, and the handwriting was often small. The title of the book and the name of the author were given at the end, if at all.

Nothing seems to be known about publishing, but copying must have been a regular trade, and by the fourth century B.C. bookshops were becoming numerous in Greece and students were learning from books as well as from oral teaching, which had long been the method in education. Many educated people must have had libraries, and a great scholar such as Aristotle must have had a large library.

When the Greek King, Alexander the Great, conquered Egypt he founded the city of Alexandria, in 331 B.C., and this soon became one of the greatest centres of Greek culture. Here a very famous library was founded by King Ptolemy I and enlarged by Ptolemy II. It was apparently the largest library since that formed by Assur-bani-pal at Nineveh, and it may have contained as many as 600,000 scrolls. It became a great centre of learning to which students came from many countries, for it set out to collect the best editions of all important Greek, Latin, Egyptian and Indian books. It seems clear that a thriving book trade must soon have developed.

When Julius Caesar burnt the Egyptian fleet in the harbour of Alexandria in 48 B.C. thousands of books stored near the harbour were burned also. Mark Antony made this good, in part at least, when he presented Cleopatra, Queen of Egypt, with the library of Pergamon, which may have contained 200,000 scrolls on parchment and papyrus. But the Alexandrian library was finally destroyed in A.D. 394, when the Roman Emperor Theodosius set fire to the city. With the books perished also all records of the book trade.

Long before this papyrus had found a rival, *parchment*, which was made from animal skins. These had been used occasionally to make writing material, at least as early as 1500 B.C., but it seems that parchment did not begin to come into regular use until the second century B.C.

The story goes that at that time Eumenes, King of Pergamon in Asia Minor, wanted to make his library even more splendid and famous than the great library of Alexandria, so he ordered large quantities of papyrus, to make books. But the Ptolemy who was ruling Egypt then was so jealous that he prohibited the export. Eumenes had to find another material and parchment was chosen. It was made from the skins of cattle, sheep and goats, and for the finest parchment, known as *vellum*, the skins of young calves, lambs and kids were used. The skins were thoroughly cleaned, all the hair was scraped off, they were rubbed smooth with pumice and then they were dressed with chalk. This produced a material which was smooth, flexible and very durable; the best writing material ever invented. All the most beautiful manuscripts have been written on it, and vellum is still used today for illuminated addresses and Books of Remembrance which are to be given the greatest dignity and permanence. Yet it was not until the fourth century A.D. that parchment really began to take the place of papyrus in general use, presumably because papyrus was so plentiful, cheap and popular.

The Latin name *charta pergamena* is derived from Pergamon, and our word *parchment*, which comes from the Latin, is a monument to King Eumenes. No one knows how many of his books were on papyrus, how many were on

Scrolls of papyrus or parchment and writing materials used in Greece and Rome. The labels attached to the scrolls give their titles. On the left are two pens and an inkwell. The things which look like books are wooden tablets covered with wax and hinged together. For writing on the wax a short rod with a sharp metal point, called a stylus, was used and two of these, with small knobs at the ends, are shown in the drawing

parchment, but they came to number some 200,000, and constituted another of the great libraries of history.

The Romans conquered Greece and Egypt in the second and first centuries B.C., but long before that, about the seventh century B.C., they had taken the Greek letters and adapted them to form the Roman alphabet which they used throughout their long history and which we use today.

The Romans wrote on papyrus, wax tablets, and parchment. The Roman papyrus scroll was very similar to the Greek, and no easier to handle and read. The words were still run together, and reading the small writing was sometimes a severe strain on the eyes.

From the first century B.C. the Romans showed a growing interest in books, and some began to form private libraries. A book trade then developed rapidly. The first or one of the first successful publishers of whom we have any record was a wealthy banker, author and scholar named Titus Pomponius Atticus (109–32 B.C.), the friend and publisher of the great orator Cicero. Like the other publishers of the time, he produced books quickly, cheaply and in large numbers by using well-educated slaves, one of whom read a manuscript aloud while the others wrote copies—a method followed later in Christian monasteries. Atticus built up a large publishing and bookselling business in Rome and the provinces. His books became famous, as *Attikians*, for their quality and accuracy.

Not all the publisher-booksellers were so scrupulous. Some books were full of mistakes; sometimes a popular author's name was put on an inferior work by an unknown writer, to make it sell. (This happened also to Shakespeare.) And since there was no copyright some authors cheated by copying other authors' work.

There were no reviews or advertisements in periodicals, but new books were given publicity by being recited or read aloud at the public recitations which drew large crowds, and their titles were posted up on the pillars outside book-shops. But no doubt the best of all publicity, then as now, was personal recommendation by one reader to another.

As soon as books became important and influential a new evil appeared—political and religious censorship. Augustus had books which he thought objectionable confiscated even from private houses, and publicly burned. Some later Emperors followed suit, and censorship has continued at intervals ever since, as it does in totalitarian countries today.

Rome superseded Alexandria as the Empire's chief book-trade centre in the latter half of the first century A.D., and books became so fashionable in Greek and Roman society that satirists, such as Martial and Lucian, ridiculed those rich men who really cared nothing for books, but collected them as what we should now call "status symbols". "If you were decked in manuscripts from head to foot," wrote Lucian, "would you be less ignorant than you are?" But there were, of course, many sincere booklovers, and in Rome, Athens and elsewhere the book-shops became favourite meeting-places for authors and readers. No doubt the first books brought into Britain were published in Rome.

The first public library in Rome was founded late in the first century B.C., by Asinius Pollio. Augustus soon founded others, and by the second century A.D. there were between twenty and thirty libraries in the city which were open to the public.

The great increase in publishing and reading brought fame to many authors, but not always fortune. There seems to be no evidence that they were regularly paid by the publisher-booksellers. The best thing they could hope for was to find wealthy patrons—which was the position in England until the late eighteenth century. The Emperor Augustus and his rich friend Maecenas were so generous to Vergil and Horace that these great poets were able to live in comfort and write what they wished. Many others were far less fortunate.

Literature and the book trade decayed with the decay of the Roman empire, and in 330 A.D. the capital was removed from Rome to Constantinople.

A large library was formed later in Constantinople (now Istanbul); but much of this was destroyed by the Crusaders in 1204 and by the Turks when they captured the city in 1453.

Throughout the long history of the ancient Greek and Roman world the papyrus scroll was the most important book-form, as it had been for many centuries before that in Egypt and neighbouring countries. Papyrus remained in general use, along with parchment, until the ninth century A.D. It was used, belatedly, for a bull (papal edict) issued by Pope Leo IX in A.D. 1051.

While papyrus was giving place to parchment as the chief writing material the scroll was also being slowly superseded, by the *codex*, which was invented about 100 A.D. It was made by folding a long strip of papyrus concertina fashion, instead of rolling it, or by folding small sheets down the middle and fitting them into each other. Perhaps both methods were used. When the back edges were sewn together this made up something which in its shape and construction was virtually the same as the modern book. It was naturally far more convenient to turn over pages than to unroll and roll up a long scroll, so *codices* were soon widely used, and all the early Christian writings were in this form. But it was centuries before the codex completely superseded the scroll. Then for a thousand years the codex of parchment or vellum became the dominant book form of Europe and the Mediterranean world, until it was superseded in its turn by the printed book.

The Dead Sea Scrolls

Early in 1947 a party of desert Arabs, possibly smugglers, were making their way through the desolate mountain country west of the Dead Sea, in order to get into

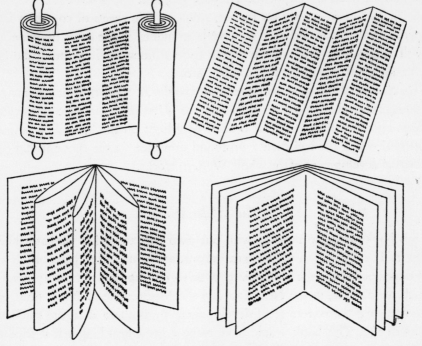

How the scroll (top left) probably developed into the codex

Palestine (as it was then). A boy named Muhammed adh Dhib, who was looking after their goats, went in search of one which had strayed and noticed a cave in a hillside. He threw a stone into it and heard something smash, which made him so curious that he came back later with another boy to explore the cave. They found a number of tall clay jars, with lids, which contained rolls with strange writing on them, wrapped in linen and smelling very nasty. They took three rolls back to their tribe, who carried them to Bethlehem and tried to sell them in the market there. After many misadventures the scrolls were bought by the head of the Syrian Monastery of St. Mark, in Jerusalem, and there followed great arguments among scholars and archaeologists as to whether the scrolls were ancient or fairly modern, genuine or forged. The cave was found with other manuscripts, and a search discovered several other caves containing large numbers of manuscripts, many in fragments. They are religious books written in Hebrew or Aramaic or Greek, mostly on leather, some on thin sheets of copper, a few on papyrus, and they are believed to have been hidden in the caves by members of Jewish religious sects who were fleeing from Roman soldiers during the Jewish revolt against Rome in the first century A.D.

This is one of the most sensational discoveries of modern times. Some of the fragments are a thousand years older than the oldest Bible manuscript ever known before, and they throw a great deal of new light on the history of religion in Palestine, which has had such a profound influence on the thought and feeling and social development of the whole Western world.

The Wider World

In this book we are concerned with our own past and what we have inherited from it. The civilisation of Western Europe, and many other parts of the world, has developed from the civilisations which grew up, and the many inventions which were made, in the Near East and the Mediterranean. But it must not be forgotten that there were great developments in southern Asia, the Far East and America also. This book would have to be a great deal longer if it tried to do justice to these other civilisations, with their very varied systems of writing, writing materials and manuscripts.

But the oldest known forms of printing must be mentioned. In Japan, in the eighth century A.D., paper charms were produced by printing, and it is thought that the art of printing may have come to Japan from China. At all events the earliest printed book which we know was found along with other documents in a cave in Szechuan in China, in A.D. 1900. This book, known as the Diamond Sutra, was printed from wooden blocks in A.D. 868 and it is therefore about six hundred years earlier than the first European printed books. Scholars think that there must have been books in China long before this, for the Diamond Sutra is beautifully printed and is certainly not the first fumbling attempt of printers trying out a new technique.

The earliest Chinese books were printed from blocks—that is to say, all the characters were cut on one block of wood, which was then inked and impressed

Part of the Diamond Sutra, the first printed book known. It was printed in China in A.D. 868, from wood blocks

on paper. In the eleventh century, still long before the appearance of printing in the West, a man named Pi-Sheng invented a means of printing from movable types. Each character was made separately from earthenware, but a whole page was printed at one time by fitting all the separate pieces together (as in modern printing) and printing from them as if from a single block. The invention was later to be of great importance to the West, but unfortunately this method is not suited to Chinese, since the language needed then (as it does still) an enormous number of different characters, ideographs. The idea of printing with movable types was therefore abandoned in China after Pi-Sheng's death. A similar method was tried in Korea, about 1390, but again it was given up.

After the collapse of the Roman Empire the monasteries became more and more the main centres of learning in Europe and were, for several centuries, almost the sole producers of books, since few people outside the Church were able to read or write. This meant that most of the *manuscripts*, handwritten books, were copies of religious works or of the writings of classical Greece and Rome which were sanctioned by the Church.

The monks spent long hours faithfully copying the sacred works in the *scriptorium*, as the writing-room of the monastery was called. At first strict silence was observed and if a monk wanted anything he had to use signs to indicate his needs to his fellows; if, for example, he wanted a pagan manuscript he had to scratch his ear like a dog! Eventually the rule of strict silence was probably relaxed so that they could adopt the Roman method of making several copies at once by setting one monk to read out the text while others wrote it down. The work could only be done during the hours of daylight, since torches or candles were not used in the scriptorium for fear of starting a fire amongst the precious manuscripts. Great accuracy in copying was insisted on, for it was, of course, essential to have true copies of the holy writings. The monks were therefore instructed to follow their originals faithfully, even when they contained an obvious mistake. Nevertheless it is not surprising that, after hours of exacting labour, the monks sometimes became inaccurate, errors crept into their work, and words were abbreviated, so that the manuscripts were difficult to read and the texts became corrupt.

As they believed that it was their duty to God to make their copies of the sacred writings as fine and as beautiful as they possibly could, they often decorated the manuscripts with coloured initials or borders. Long before, in the papyrus rolls of ancient Egypt, the initial letter of a paragraph had often been coloured red for emphasis, a practice which we call *rubricating*. Now in the monasteries manuscripts might be treated in the same way. Initial letters were enlarged and coloured and as time went by they became more and more ornate. The important initials at the beginning of the Gospels or the Psalms were decorated with intertwining foliage and animals and were often made to fill the whole page. Tiny pictures were drawn within the frames of letters like Q and B. Grotesque animals, and sometimes even little men, were distorted to the shape of the appropriate initial. Elaborate borders of foliage with animals and birds and little scenes were introduced. The monks used for illustrations all the plants and animals which they saw in the fields and woods near the monastery, and, not content with drawing real animals, they would invent all kinds of strange creatures, mythical, symbolical or purely imaginary. In some manuscripts every page is swarming with decorations of this kind, each one minute and exquisitely painted. Miniature pictures two or three inches square were painted to illustrate scenes described in the text, and the most handsome volumes of all have full-page illustrations as well, usually contained within wide ornamental borders of foliage and flowers. The colours which the monks loved most were bright reds and blues, highlighted with shining gold, and smaller quantities of green, yellow and purple. Small wonder that books decorated with these brilliant colours are known as *illuminated manuscripts*. It is hard to believe that such gay and lively designs have been painted in the religious quiet of the great monasteries.

Some of the finest manuscripts were produced in Ireland and the north of England in the monasteries of the Celtic church. The famous *Lindisfarne Gospels* were written and illuminated for Eadfrith, the Bishop of Lindisfarne, an island off the coast of Northumbria, probably about A.D. 698. The manuscript is still in good condition, in spite of the fact that it is said to have been dropped into the sea when a later bishop was crossing to Ireland to escape from an invasion of Vikings. Luckily it was found again at low tide by the aid of a miracle. The

A single word from a page of the Lindisfarne Gospels, greatly enlarged

Lindisfarne Gospels are decorated with complicated interlacing designs, large ornamental initials and a wealth of abstract pattern. Even the portraits of the four
Evangelists are made to look stiffly ornamental.

The *Book of Kells*, which is believed to have been made in Ireland about a
century later, has been called the most beautiful book in the world. The text is
superbly written in a fine, regular hand, adorned with little designs in colour.
The decoration is so elaborate that it is traditionally supposed to have been traced
by the angels, and indeed the intricate patterns, the grotesque animals and the
strange colour combinations are the work of an imagination utterly foreign to the
twentieth-century mind.

The bindings of these manuscripts were often elaborate and sometimes very
costly, for even the finest bindings were considered hardly good enough to en-
shrine the Word of God. So they were bound in heavy wooden boards covered
with precious metal inlaid with jewels, or with leather richly decorated in gold
or colour, which was impressed into the leather with metal stamps. Often these
books were closed with metal clasps, which could be locked, and were attached
by a chain to the library shelf so that they could not be removed from the monastery. You can still see a few chained books of this kind in certain university
libraries, and there are still several old chained libraries in Britain, at Wimborne
Minster and Guildford Grammar School, for example.

As time went by manuscripts were made more and more decorative and the
skills required in making them became more specialised, and several monks
collaborated on one manuscript. One prepared the parchment for writing on,
another copied out the text, leaving spaces for borders and decorated initials
which were added by a third, while a fourth painted the illustrations and a fifth
made the binding.

Eventually, in Britain and all over Europe, manuscripts came to be valued, not
only as books containing the Word of God, but as objects which were beautiful
to look at. This meant that they could be sold outside, enabling the monasteries
to acquire more land and property in exchange. More manuscripts were therefore
produced for sale, and lay scribes had to be employed to keep up with the increasing demand. Craftsmen were brought in from outside for special jobs such
as painting the elaborate initials.

A page from an eleventh century manuscript copy of Caedmon's Poems. The whole story of Noah's Ark is told in this drawing – at the bottom Noah and his wife enter the ark; in the middle the animals are happily settled, and at the top Noah is sending out the dove after the flood has subsided

These manuscripts were bought by noblemen who liked to possess beautiful books, and by the wealthier scholars. Most of the books made for the new patrons were still religious books such as Psalters and Breviaries, but the text was often no more than an excuse for fine illumination. A particularly popular type in Europe during the fourteenth and fifteenth centuries was the *Book of Hours*, so-called because it contained the "Hours" of the Virgin, services which were said or sung at certain hours of the day. These offered a wonderful opportunity for the artist, since they contained a variety of prayers, Gospel lessons, Psalms and a calendar, which were usually accompanied by miniatures and by exquisite decorations. The section containing the calendar, for example, was illustrated by twelve miniatures, one for each month, depicting typical seasonal occupations: hunting, feasting, ploughing, harvesting, grape-picking, and so on.

Sometimes, instead of having frames or borders, the margins of a page were filled with informal sketches depicting scenes from everyday life, often quite unconnected with the text, a kind of inspired doodling. One of the finest examples is the manuscript made about 1330 which later became *Queen Mary's Psalter* because it was used by Queen Mary of England, and is now in the British Museum. Many of its illustrations are outline drawings shaded with a wash of transparent colour, a style in which English artists from the eleventh century onwards excelled.

Besides luxury books painted by artists for the rich there were popular books produced in large quantities to a set pattern, for by the thirteenth century secular books were becoming more common. People wanted more amusing books, as well as the religious and classical works which had been produced by the monasteries for the use of the Church. There was now a demand for *romances*, long adventure stories in verse or prose, such as the Tales of King Arthur and his Knights; for *bestiaries*, which were collections of moral tales and strange lore about various animals, some real, some mythical; and for *herbals*, which contained instructions for making medicines from plants and herbs. In the fifteenth century stories and poems, such as Chaucer's *Canterbury Tales*, were common, and histories were particularly popular. Because they were produced in large quantities, and had to be quickly made, they were often very simply and even roughly, illustrated, a far cry from the beautiful illuminated manuscripts described earlier.

A wood block printed page of a fifteenth century Biblia Pauperum

Other methods of reproducing books more quickly were being tried out during the fifteenth century. *Block printing*, which had been used for some time for printing patterns on cloth and for making playing cards, was now used to produce religious images, and eventually whole books as well. The design which was to be printed was drawn or traced in reverse on a smooth block of wood. The wood was then cut away to leave the design standing out in relief. This was covered with printing ink and pressed face downwards on to paper, printing the image the right way round. A large number of copies could be printed from this block, but a great deal of patience and skill was needed to cut a design in wood, especially if it contained many words as well as pictures, and a separate block had to be made for every page of a book. Letters are small and intricate and it must have been very difficult to cut them out of wood. For this reason many block books consist almost entirely of pictures with perhaps a sentence of writing underneath to explain them. Some of the most popular books of this kind were the *Biblia Pauperum*, the Poor Man's Bibles, which consisted of series of pictures telling the well-known Bible stories. People in the pictures often had to be labelled to show who they were, and sometimes words were drawn coming out of their mouths in "balloons", just as in the comic strips in newspapers today. Usually there was also a sentence of explanation under the picture, but on the whole as little lettering as possible was used. This was not a disadvantage, since few people could read in any case. There were also block books which contained a great deal of text, but the letters were heavy and very clumsy. These books were issued in large numbers during the fifteenth and sixteenth centuries, even after the invention of printing from movable types.

Paper

While books were written on parchment they could never be produced cheaply or in large quantities, since parchment is made from animal skins, and the supply of these is naturally limited. Think how many would be needed to make enough parchment for a single edition of a best-seller today! Fortunately, in the fifteenth century, when more people were beginning to read books, another material—paper—was available.

The Chinese discovered how to make paper, perhaps as early as A.D. 104.

A papermaker at work. Through the window you can see water-wheels which work the paddles which beat the cloth rags in the trough under the window. The pulp is transferred to the vat in the foreground. The papermaker has removed some of the pulp in his sieve to make a sheet of paper. (From a German book of the sixteenth century)

However that may be, they certainly knew how to make paper many centuries before the craft was brought to Europe.

In the eighth century the Chinese taught the Arabs how to make paper when the Arabs conquered Tartary, one of the western provinces of China. At this time the Arabs spread far beyond the Arabian peninsula in their eagerness to convert the world to the Moslem faith, and everywhere they went they introduced the Arab civilisation, which was in many ways more advanced than that of the peoples whom they conquered. They occupied the Middle East and North Africa, crossed the Straits of Gibraltar and conquered Spain, where they remained until 1492.

The Arabs manufactured paper at Jativa in Spain during the eleventh century. By 1283 a paper mill, probably the first in the Christian world, had been set up at Fabriano in Italy. Gradually the rest of Europe also learned how to make paper and by 1490, two centuries later, the first English paper mill was working.

In Europe paper was usually made from linen rags, which were washed, steeped in water, and then reduced to a pulp. This was diluted with more water and the liquid mixture was then poured into a tray with a flat bottom made of wire mesh. The water drained off between the wires leaving a sheet of matted fibres which was hung over a rope and when dry became a sheet of paper.

At first little interest was shown in the new material, since it was neither as strong nor as beautiful as parchment. But eventually, when more books were wanted, the supply of parchment became inadequate and paper had to be used instead. If this material had not been available, even the invention of printing could not have greatly increased the production of books.

The Invention of Printing

Before the invention of printing books were expensive and only the rich could afford to buy them. This meant that education was almost entirely confined to the rich and the scholar-clerics. As there were no newspapers and few books, most people knew little of the world beyond their own parish.

Because it made possible the spread of knowledge and ideas, printing is one of the most important inventions in the history of the world—and yet we are not sure who first invented the process, or when. The idea of printing may have originated independently in Europe, or it may have come from China, as paper did. The Chinese were printing books by the ninth century A.D., as we have seen, and printing did not appear in Europe until after the famous Venetian traveller, Marco Polo (1254–1324), and others, had returned from the Far East full of the wonders they had found. About the middle of the fifteenth century the demand for books in Europe was increasing and we know that several people in different European countries were trying to find a way of producing books mechanically. Block books were familiar, and could be printed reasonably quickly *once the blocks had been cut*, but cutting them was a long and laborious business, and of course they could be used only for the book for which they had been made.

It is generally believed that John Gutenberg, working during the 1430s, first at Strassburg and then at Mainz in Germany, was the first to print from movable types in the Western world. Gutenberg had been a goldsmith, and he applied his knowledge of fine metalwork to the casting of metal type. He discovered how to make letters in a mould, all exactly alike. He then combined the separate letters, or types, to form words and sentences. When he had assembled all the types necessary for a whole page of print he clamped them together in a frame and printed them all at once, just as if they were a single block. When the block was no longer needed the frame could be unlocked and the type used again for something completely different. It was essential that the type be made with great precision so that all the letters would fit together neatly and securely in the frame, and make an even printing surface, and Gutenberg was the first to discover a method of making type accurately enough for this.

In order to print a page the frame containing the type was laid face upwards on the flat bed of the printing press, an adapted version of the winepress which had been used for many centuries. The type was inked by rubbing it with large leather balls covered with a special printing ink. The sheet of paper to be printed was carefully placed in position over the type and the heavy plate of the press was screwed down on top of it. When the screw was released the printed paper was taken out and another blank sheet laid in position.

In order to save time and work, two, four or eight pages were printed at once on the same sheet of paper, and the paper was then folded, and cut to the required page size.

This method was a great deal quicker than writing out every copy of a book by hand, and it was also a great deal more accurate, since every copy was exactly the same as the others.

The earliest printed document which has so far come to light is an Indulgence

The printing press. In the background two compositors are setting up the type. In the foreground you can see the printing press itself. One man is inking the type while the other removes a printed sheet from the press. On the right is the heavy metal plate which is screwed down to press the paper on to the type. (From a German book of the sixteenth century)

printed by Gutenberg at Mainz in 1454. In the following year he printed another Indulgence, and at the same time he must have been working on the first book printed from movable type—a Bible which appeared in 1455, and is now famous as "the Gutenberg Bible". Part of a page of this Bible is shown in the frontispiece.

Knowledge of the techniques of printing spread rapidly, for many of the early German printers learnt the business and then travelled to other countries to set up their presses. Books were being printed in Switzerland by 1466, Italy by 1467, France and the Netherlands by 1470, Spain by 1473 and England by 1476.

Printing was introduced into England by William Caxton, an English merchant who, while living at Bruges in the Netherlands, learned the new craft at Cologne. He set up his own press in Bruges, where he produced in 1474 the first book ever printed in English, the *Recuyell of the Histories of Troye*, which he had himself translated from the French, and other books. When he returned to England he set up a press near Westminster Abbey and in 1477 he produced the first dated book printed in England, the *Dictes or Sayengis of the Philosophers*.

He worked very fast and in the course of his energetic career he printed in all nearly a hundred works, twenty of them his own translations of French books. He also seems to have imported books from abroad and exported books to France. Although at this time continental publishers tended to concentrate on Latin editions of the classics Caxton printed a large number of books in English, for he realised that these too would sell well. He printed books which would appeal to many readers: Chaucer's *Canterbury Tales*, medieval romances such as Malory's *Morte d'Arthur*, adventure stories and other books of the same kind, as well as books on religion and philosophy. He was a man of parts, author, scholar, translator and editor, as well as printer, publisher and bookseller, and in combining a genuine love of books with business enterprise he set an example which is still followed by the best publishers today.

The earliest printers had to be their own publishers and often had to sell their books, too, as this advertisement issued by Caxton shows:

"If it please any man spiritual or temporal to buy any pyes of two or three Commemorations of the Use of Salisbury, imprinted after the form of the present letter, which are well and truly correct, let him come to Westminster to the almonry of the Red Pale and he shall have them good cheap."—That is to say, Caxton sold his books in the shop where he printed them. (See p. 78 for a reproduction of the advertisement.)

Besides learning to use a new process the first printers had to design their type-faces. Naturally enough these faces imitated the manuscript writing of the time,

ranne in to the forst / And whanne the wyldr beestes sawe
hym come / they were so ferdfull that they alle beganne to flee /
For they wendr / that it hadr be the lyon / And the mayster of
the asse serched and soughte his asse in euery place al aboute
And as he hadr soughte longe / he thought that he wolde go in
to the forst for to see yf his asse were there / And as soone as

A page from Caxton's Aesop's Fables, printed at Westminster in 1483

not because they wanted to deceive anyone into thinking that their printed books
were manuscripts, but simply because people would only buy books which looked
like the manuscripts they were accustomed to. So the first typefaces were based

on the heavy and closely woven *black letter* or *gothic* handwriting, which was decorative, but was very difficult to read, as you can see if you look at Caxton's advertisement on p. 78. *Roman* type was first cut in 1467 and is so called because it is based on letters first used in manuscripts in Rome. Fortunately for us it was favoured by the great Venetian printer, Aldus Manutius, whose books became well known all over Europe and made roman more popular than black letter. The book which you are now reading is printed in a roman typeface, Monotype Bembo, a modern version of one of Manutius' types.

Quia noueram mores hominum ;tum
etiam pertentare te prorfus uolui ,q̃ recte
ifta fentires. Sed omittamus haec iam tan
dem filî ; atq; ad eam partem fermonis,
ex qua egreffi fumus, reuertamur.

De Aetna, printed in 1495 in the handsome Bembo type
designed for Aldus Manutius by Francesco Griffo.
The type in which this book is printed is a modern
version of Bembo

Very soon after the invention of printing, in 1494, Aldus Manutius set up his press in Venice and started to print the first pocket books. He was a scholar, anxious to revive interest in classical learning by making Greek and Latin texts widely available at the lowest possible prices. In order to do this he printed large editions of his books, and made them small in size.

A very compact typeface was specially designed so that more words could be fitted into a page. *This type, the type in which this sentence is printed, we now call italic.*

Fifteenth-century printed books (which are now known as *incunabula*) looked more like manuscripts than like the books of today. Not only was the type designed to look like handwriting, there was no title page, and the printer's name and the place and date of printing were given at the end, in imitation of the scribes who signed their names at the end of manuscripts. Often the author's name was not given at all, for this was not thought to be important unless the author was particularly well known. The first page was left completely blank as a protective

N ec sum adeo informis, nuper me in littore uidi,
C um placidum uentis staret mare. non ego Daphnin
I udice te metuam, si nunquam fallat imago·
O tantum libeat mecum tibi sordida rura,
A tq; humileis habitare casas, & figere ceruos,
O edorum'q; gregem uiridi compellere hibisco·
M ecum una in syluis imitabere Pana canendo.
P an primus calamos cæra coniungere plures
I nstituit, Pan curat oues, ouium'q; magistros.
N ec te pœniteat calamo triuisse labellum·
H æc eadem ut sciret, quid non faciebat, Amyntas?
E st mihi disparibus septem compacta cicutis
F istula, Damœtas dono mihi quam dedit olim,
E t dixit moriens, te nunc habet ista secundum·
D ixit Damœtas, inuidit stultus Amyntas.
P ræterea duo nec tuta mihi ualle reperti
C apreoli, sparsis etiam nunc pellibus albo,
B ina die siccant ouis ubera, quos tibi seruo.
I am pridem à me illos abducere Thestylis orat·
E t faciet· quoniam sordent tibi munera nostra.
H uc ades o formose puer· tibi lilia plenis
E cce ferunt nymphæ calathis, tibi candida Nais
P allentes uiolas, et summa papauera carpens,
N arcissum, et florem iungit bene olentis anethi,
T um casia, atq; alijs intexens suauibus herbis,
M ollia luteola pingit uacinia caltha·
I pse ego cana legam tenera lanugine mala,
C astaneas'q; nuces, mea quas Amaryllis amabat·
A ddam cærea pruna, et honos erit huic quoq; pomo·
E t uos o lauri carpam· & te proxima myrte,

a iiii

A page of one of the cheap editions of the classics published by
Aldus Manutius using the specially-designed compact italic type

cover for the book, as books were usually sold unbound. Most people liked to
have their books bound to their own requirements after they had bought them,
perhaps to match the other books in their library. Later, the title was printed on
the blank front page so that it acted as a kind of label. By the beginning of the

sixteenth century the publisher-booksellers realised that this "title page" could act as an advertisement, attracting a prospective customer's attention by decorative woodcut borders or a striking picture, just as the colourful covers of paperbacks today attract our attention and make us want to buy them. The title page at this period often carried a description of the contents of the book, the sort of information which we would now expect to find on the dust-jacket.

Many of the early printed books were illustrated by woodcuts like those of the block books. Sometimes, to save work, the same woodcuts were used again and again, and a picture of a city might appear first as Rome, a few pages later as Paris, and further on again as Jerusalem, or, indeed, as any other city which happened to be mentioned in the text.

At first wealthy book collectors looked down on printed books, and some refused to have anything but manuscripts in their libraries. Nevertheless some of the books produced during the first century of printing are among the finest ever printed and they are regarded as priceless treasures by book collectors today. Although they were experimenting with a new process the early printers used it with great mastery, and we still copy the typefaces which they designed, for they have never been bettered.

The Book Trade Develops

Very soon after the invention of printing, presses were set up in every country in Europe. It was, however, three hundred years before any more important technical developments were made.

This does not mean, of course, that the new industry stood still. On the contrary, it became much more highly organised: presses were devised which could print larger sheets of paper; printers used more presses, so that they could have more work under way at one time; and, most important, the increase in trade meant that one man could no longer undertake the whole business of printing, publishing and selling a book, and so each process became a specialised trade. First of all the printer and the publisher-bookseller separated. Then during the seventeenth century bookshops were gradually taken over by independent booksellers, and were no longer managed by the publishers as they had been hitherto. The publisher became more important, organising and co-ordinating the various

stages of production and distribution. In short, the book trade slowly developed
from the one-man business that it had been in Caxton's day to the complicated
and highly specialised organisation that we have today.

To us it seems extraordinary that authors in the early days of printing did not
expect payment for their books—or at least they did not expect to be paid by the
publisher. Instead, the author dedicated his work to a rich nobleman who would
grant him some favour in return—a cash reward, perhaps, or a better job. This
system, known as *patronage*, died out in the eighteenth century, when publishers
could afford to pay for the work they published, and so authors no longer had to
rely on favours from the rich.

With the invention of printing books became cheaper and easier to get, more
people could afford to buy them and so they played an increasingly important
part in spreading ideas and knowledge. This meant that books could be used
as powerful propaganda. To prevent the publication of unorthodox ideas a censorship was exercised. The Churches suppressed writings which they regarded as
heretical and governments suppressed books which criticised them. The first list
of books which were banned in England was issued in 1529 by Henry VIII. In
order to avoid the censorship controversial books were often printed in the
Netherlands or elsewhere and then smuggled into England; or if they were
printed in England the printer put a false name and address on the books, so that
he could not be traced and punished. During the troubled reigns of Henry VIII,
Mary, Elizabeth and the Stuart kings many religious and political books were
published in this way. The poet Milton was so angered by the Puritan censorship
that in 1644 he wrote an address to Parliament, the famous *Areopagitica*, in which
he argued for the complete freedom of the Press. It was not until 1695, however,
that the Press in England was finally released from Government control, and in
totalitarian countries there is still a strict political censorship.

The invention of printing meant also that news could be spread much more
quickly than ever before, and towards the end of the eighteenth century newspapers and periodicals became increasingly important, and began to develop
rapidly.

We have seen that in the earliest days of printing there were three different
kinds of letter: gothic or blackletter, italic and roman. After the beginning of the

THE CASTLE

OF

OTRANTO

A

GOTHIC STORY, &c.

CHAPTER I.

*M*ANFRED, Prince of *Otranto*, had one son and one daughter: The latter a most beautiful virgin, aged eighteen, was called *Matilda*. *Conrad*, the son, was three years younger, a homely youth, sickly, and of no promising disposition; yet he was the darling of his father, who never showed any symptoms of affection to *Matilda*. *Manfred* had contracted a marriage for his son with the Marquis of *Vicenza*'s daughter,

A page printed in Bodoni's new face type with very marked contrast between the thick and thin strokes. This book was printed in Parma in 1791 for J. Edwards, a London publisher-bookseller

seventeenth century gothic type was very little used except in Germany, where it is only now beginning to die out. Italic, which was designed for printing compact pocket books, was, after the sixteenth century, used only in combination with roman type, for emphasis, or simply as a contrast, for anything printed entirely in italic is difficult to read.

Roman, then, became the principal typeface for books and many different roman faces have been designed. At first these were based on handwriting, but during the eighteenth century type designers began to think that type ought not to imitate letters written with a pen, but ought rather to show that they were cut in metal, so they designed letters which were sharper and more regular in form. John Baskerville, a printer who produced his first book at Birmingham in 1757, paid particular attention to the appearance of his books, and he designed one of the first typefaces which did not imitate letters written with a pen. This typeface, called *Baskerville* after its author, is still very popular in this country. The trend started by Baskerville was carried to its logical conclusion by the Italian typographer Giambattista Bodoni (1740–1813). He designed a typeface which immediately suggests that it is cut in metal, for the thin strokes, as you see, are very fine indeed, and the contrast between the thick and thin strokes is very marked.

Most English books today, however, are printed in typefaces modelled on those of the sixteenth century.

During the fifteenth and sixteenth centuries many famous artists designed illustrations for books, Albrecht Dürer and Hans Holbein amongst them. The artist's sketch was engraved in wood or metal by a craftsman, and the illustration printed from this engraving. The success of an illustration made in this way depended very much on the engraver's skill as well as on the original artist. Colour was not often used in illustrations until the nineteenth century, as colour printing was difficult, and indeed it was cheaper to print a book with the illustrations in outline and then paint in the colours by hand afterwards.

A wood engraving by Thomas Bewick

The woodcut had fallen out of favour by the eighteenth century and was little used until Thomas Bewick (1753–1828) made it popular again with his charming and lively decorations depicting country scenes, animals and birds.

Many fine books were produced during the seventeenth and eighteenth centuries, but printing methods and tools remained almost unchanged. Then, after the end of the eighteenth century, rapid technical progress was made.

Technical Progress

In the nineteenth century, the age of industrial revolution, when machines were invented to do many things which had previously been done by hand, printing like many other trades was greatly changed by the new processes introduced.

Before the nineteenth century paper was made entirely by hand, but in 1799 a Frenchman patented a paper-making machine. The Fourdrinier machine, as it was called after the inventor, could make paper ten times as quickly as even the best craftsmen using the old methods, and instead of small sheets it produced a continuous roll of paper many feet wide.

Hand-made paper had always been made from cloth rags, but by 1840 there were simply not enough cloth rags to provide paper for all the books and newspapers which were being printed. Some other material had to be found. As early as 1719 it had been discovered that wood could be used, and during the nineteenth century it was used more and more. Paper-making is now a major industry in well-forested countries like Sweden, Finland, and Canada, although, of course, a great deal of paper, particularly paper for books, is still made in Britain. Esparto grass, which grows in Spain and North Africa, also provides fibre which can be mixed with other materials to make paper, and this was first used by *The Times* in 1854.

At the same time people were working on methods of improving the printing press itself. The first big step forward was made by Earl Stanhope, about 1800, when he introduced an iron press which was quicker and easier to handle than the old wooden ones, and it could also print larger sheets of paper, but it was still worked by hand. Then, on the 29th of November 1814, *The Times* was printed on a press which worked by steam power. At first this press, invented by

Friedrich Konig, was used only for newspapers, since book printers thought that it could not possibly produce the best work. Eventually, twelve years after it was first introduced by *The Times*, an enterprising printer of Leipzig in Germany started to use it for books as well, and gradually others followed his example.

One of the slowest and most complicated of all the processes of printing is the setting up of type, which involved picking the letters one by one out of the type case, placing them in their correct position in the page of type, and then putting them back in the right compartment of the type case after the book had been printed. For centuries this had to be done by hand, just as it was in Gutenberg's day. People had tried for many years to think of some way of mechanising type-setting, but no one had had any success. Machines had been invented which were much faster than human compositors, but they could not put the type back in the type case, so boys still had to finish off the job. The problem was solved at last, however, and in a completely unexpected way, when the American, Otto Mergenthaler, invented the Linotype in 1886. This machine sets up the type by casting it from molten metal, making a whole line of type in a single piece. It was this which gave the machine its name. All the operator has to do is to tap out the letters on a keyboard rather like a typewriter. When the printing is finished the type is simply melted down and the metal is used again. Many printers, however, do not like the rigid line of type for book printing, and prefer to have individually cast letters instead, so they use the Monotype machine which was invented a few years later, in 1889, by an American called Tolbert Lanston. The Monotype is similar to the Linotype except that it makes every letter separately, as in the old days of hand printing. Both of these, and the Intertype, another machine of similar kind, work much faster than a human compositor. The fact that they use type which is always freshly made, not old and worn, is another very important advantage.

The technical advances made in the printing industry during the nineteenth century were very great, and work could be produced much more quickly and in larger quantities than ever before. Nevertheless, if Caxton were to walk into a modern book-printing works he would soon feel at home. He would be puzzled by a Monotype machine, of course, but he would recognise the types which it makes, for they are much the same as hand-made ones. It may be, however, that in the future metal types will not be used at all. It is now possible to compose print by photographic means, replacing metal types by photographic images. This is a new process with exciting possibilities which are still being developed and explored, but even now photosetting machines are being used commercially for all kinds of work, and already a few books have been printed in this way. Because film is used instead of metal the "type" for a whole book can be packed away in a briefcase, whereas metal type for the same book would weigh about a ton!

Besides speeding up the production of paper and the printing of books, machines have also made illustrations and binding cheaper.

Until the end of the eighteenth century the publisher usually sent his books unbound to the bookseller. When someone bought a book he would tell the bookseller what sort of binding he wanted, and the bookseller would then have it done for him by a craftsman. Only the cheapest books, which were not worthy of an expensive tailor-made binding, were given some kind of protective cover before being sent to the bookseller. By 1820, however, books were more often bound in cloth instead of leather. Then machines were invented to make cloth cases and attach them to the books. The result looks very much like a hand-bound book, but it is not nearly so strong, so we call the process *casing*, not binding.

Not long after cased books arrived on the scene someone thought it would be a good idea to give them an extra paper wrapper to protect the casing and prevent it from fading in the bookshop. This wrapper, or *dust-jacket*, became common by 1890 and soon it was made to be an advertisement for the book: it was printed with an eye-catching design and information about the book and its author was given on the flaps and the back cover.

Until the nineteenth century books seldom had coloured illustrations, for they were expensive and difficult to print, but in 1796 an Austrian, Aloysius Senefelder, invented lithography (explained on page 75)—a method of printing illustrations which is especially suitable for colour work. Lithography really means drawing on stone, but Senefelder later discovered that metal plates could be used in the same way. Nowadays it appears most often in children's books, but until the invention of photography nearly all coloured illustrations were lithographic.

After the middle of the nineteenth century photographs became more and more common, and for certain types of book they have almost ousted any other kind of illustration: art books, biographies and books on travel or history, for example, are nearly always illustrated by photographs. They are easy to reproduce (see pages 73-4), and represent accurately what the eye sees, and so in some ways they have certain advantages over other methods of illustration which depend on the artist's interpretation.

In this chapter we have seen the effect of new machines on paper-making, printing, binding and illustration, and we have seen how the appearance of books has changed because of the new processes. At the same time important events were taking place in other fields which also affected book production, for the Education Act of 1870 meant that more people could read than ever before.

A Wider Reading Public

In 1870, then, the Elementary Education Act allowed for the provision of free schools in districts where they were needed. Ten years later school attendance was made compulsory. The result was that eventually more people than ever before were able to read, the poor as well as the gentry.

A great many of these new readers who were not at all interested in books frequently read newspapers and magazines. During the nineteenth century those newspapers which existed already increased their circulation enormously, and many others were started.

Authors and book publishers also were naturally eager to sell their books to the wider public, and brought out large quantities of cheap reading matter. In Victorian times novels were especially popular, and the longer they were the more people liked them. The most popular of all were those that stretched to three volumes, the "three-deckers".

People could not afford to buy this kind of book very often and so lending libraries were used more and more. They provided novels for those who wanted nothing but light entertainment, and more serious books as well for people who wanted to get ahead, and who realised that books gave them a way of educating themselves after they had left school.

Other ways were found of making books available to those who could not pay high prices. About 1900 several firms started to publish cheap reprints of well-established, safe-selling authors like Dickens and Shakespeare. The books were small in size, with a uniform binding for the whole series, and cost only sixpence or a shilling each. Although they were so cheap they made a profit for the publishers because they were printed and sold in such large numbers. In fact, the publishers were doing what Aldus Manutius had done four centuries earlier in Italy, but doing it with mass-production machinery. Everyman's Library and the World's Classics, both flourishing today, are two of several series which were started soon after 1900.

At about the same time the first book clubs began, in Switzerland, but they were not well established in Britain until the nineteen-thirties. These clubs reprint only books which have already proved to be popular, and offer them to their members at a standard price which is very much less than the original published price. The members promise to buy a certain number of the books offered, stating in advance which books they want. The publisher knows exactly how many copies to have printed, and because large sales are guaranteed he can afford to charge a low price. In Britain these clubs never reissue a book until at least two years after it is first published, for otherwise the original publisher would not be able to sell the first, more expensive edition.

The coming of the railways helped to make cheap books more popular, since even people who do not normally read much may buy a book when faced with the boredom of a long train journey, and bookstalls were soon opened at the main stations. As the book might be thrown away when finished it had to be very cheap indeed. Such cheap, compact books were invaluable during the two world wars, for they could be easily packed in a haversack and provided relaxation for the troops.

"The paperback revolution", which is described in a later chapter, has greatly increased the number of book-buyers and readers, but the greatest factor of all has been the spread of education, and the great increase in the number of people, in Britain and throughout the world, who realise that they must be educated to cope with the world of today.

Thanks to the technical advances made during the nineteenth century books can be made cheaply and in large numbers. For many years, however, hardly anyone bothered very much what their books looked like, and a great many of them were very unattractive indeed. They were badly designed, the print was difficult to read, and they were cased in shoddy material which began to fade very soon. Very thick soft paper, known as *feather-weight*, was sometimes used, to make the buyer think he was getting more for his money, and the pages of these books tended to come loose.

The low standards of commercial book production shocked William Morris, who was a craftsman, interested in all branches of design, as well as a poet. So that he could print books himself and put into practice his ideas on book design he founded the Kelmscott Press in 1890 at his house in Hammersmith, London. He worked with Emery Walker, a well-known printing technician, and together they produced fifty-three books between 1891 and 1896. Since Morris believed that nothing made by machine could be beautiful, all these books were printed with a hand press on specially commissioned hand-made paper.

Because Morris's ideas on design were inspired by the medieval manuscripts which he admired so much the Kelmscott books are printed in an archaic gothic type, with woodcut initials and heavy decorated borders. The gothic type makes his books difficult to read, and indeed they do not appear particularly beautiful to us, for our ideals have changed since Morris's time. Nevertheless the Kelmscott Press is very important in the history of book design, for it marked a turn in the tide: it was the first press set up specially to print fine books and it helped to make printers and publishers, and the general public as well, conscious of book design. Kelmscott books were, however, far too elaborate to have much direct influence on the design of commercially printed books.

The Doves Press was founded in 1900 by T. J. Cobden-Sanderson and Emery Walker in order to produce books which would be elegant, but, in contrast to the Kelmscott Press books, entirely without decoration. Their aims were therefore much nearer those of commercial book printers, but the books which they produced are much handsomer than anything else published at the time.

pains they adorned it, this unromantic, un-
eventful-looking land of England, surely by
this too our hearts may be touched and our
hope quickened.

FOR as was the land, such was the art of it while folk yet troubled themselves about such things; it strove little to impress people either by pomp or ingenuity: not unseldom it fell into commonplace, rarely it rose into majesty; yet was it never oppressive, never a slave's nightmare or an insolent boast: & at its best it had an inventiveness, an individuality, that grander styles have never overpassed: its best too, and that was in its very heart, was given as freely to the yeoman's house, and the humble village church, as to the lord's palace or the mighty cathedral: never coarse, though often rude enough, sweet, natural & unaffected, an art of peasants rather than of merchant princes or courtiers, it must be a hard heart, I think, that does not love it: whether a man has been born among it like ourselves, or has come wonder-

68

William Morris's Chaucer type

There have since been many other private presses producing a small number of books distinguished by their good design. Only a few people could afford to buy private press books, but all the same it was largely through the influence of the private presses that interest in design revived and higher standards were applied throughout the printing industry.

During the nineteen-twenties and thirties there were many signs of a new and enthusiastic approach: private presses flourished; periodicals devoted to typography were founded; many new typefaces were designed, including many specially for Monotype and Linotype machines. The most important result was that many books were now being well designed and well produced. Even some of the cheapest, such as Dent's famous *Everyman's Library*, were designed by the highest standards of the time. In 1935 Sir Allen Lane founded Penguin Books, the first really successful series of paperbacks in this country, and although they only had paper covers and sold for the astonishingly low price of sixpence, they too were attractively designed and proved that a book need not be badly produced just because it is cheap. Since 1935 standards have continued to rise. Perhaps the most striking improvements have been in school textbooks and children's books, but every kind of book has benefited. Illustrations have greatly improved also, especially illustrations in colour, thanks partly to the great public demand since the Second World War for books on art and archaeology. Only the design of binding cases has lagged behind, and many of them are still very dull. On the whole, the average British book of today is well produced, a pleasure to handle, and far more attractive and easier to read than the average book of fifty years ago, yet book prices remain lower than in all, or nearly all, other countries.

II. THE PRESENT

A Book is Written

Every book has to be written or compiled by someone; it is forged from the writer's thought and feeling. This is so obvious that it does not seem worth saying —yet it is quite often forgotten.

There is plenty of trivial writing, and most, if not all, of today's newspapers, this month's magazines and many other items of journalism and entertainment, are as quickly written as they are quickly forgotten. But creative writing—a poem, a play, a novel—if it is undertaken seriously, is one of the hardest and most difficult kinds of work which a human being can attempt, and serious writing of any kind —history or biography, science or scholarship, philosophy or criticism, for example—must often ask a great deal of the writer. It may take months or years of difficult research and hard thinking. Moreover, any serious writer may have to wrestle with questions of artistic and social conscience which affect his whole life.

Some writers, even some good ones, write easily and enjoy it; but for many writing is always painful and difficult, no matter how much they write or how successful they are. The brilliantly successful eighteenth-century dramatist R. B. Sheridan is said to have addressed these lines to an aristocratic author:

> You write with ease to show your breeding,
> But easy writing's vile hard reading.

That is often true, and when a book is clear and easy to read it is so, more often than not, because the author has laboured his hardest, criticising his work ruthlessly and rewriting it again and again.

Some people write for the joy of creative effort; some because they have something to say about life which they feel they must say; some for the satisfaction of finding out all they can about a particular subject and trying to set it down clearly; some because they are driven by an impulse which they may resent but cannot resist. Others write for fame or for money, or to get promotion in their work. Most authors write from a mixture of these motives.

When an author has completed a book he nearly always wants to get it published and usually he wants to be paid for it. Fortunately, in Britain and in other civilised countries, an author's work is now fully protected by copyright laws. No one can copy it or make use of it without his permission, because that would be a serious breach of the law. For example, a dramatic society which performs a copyright play without the author's permission is not only cheating him, it is laying itself open to proceedings in a court of law.

Any piece of original writing, from a schoolboy's essay to a great author's latest work, is automatically copyright. It does not have to be registered or published to be protected. Copyright continues for fifty years from the date of the writer's death or from the date of first publication, whichever is the later. This means, for example, that a few minor writings of Jane Austen (1775–1817) are still in copyright because they remained unpublished until 1922 or after. But nearly all her work, including all the famous novels, is out of copyright and can be freely published and used by anyone—like nearly all the works of all authors who died more than fifty years ago.

Besides national copyright laws there are international agreements which all important countries have now signed, except Russia and Communist China, so that an author's property is protected against theft nearly everywhere, and this is necessary if authors are to be paid for their labours. A book is therefore a piece of property which its author can sell or lease, in parts or as a whole; book rights, television rights, serial rights, etc., can be sold separately. Usually he thinks first of getting it published in book form.

As soon as the book is finished the author sets out to find a publisher. (A well-known author or a specialist may do this while the book is still only an idea in his head.) He may go to a literary agent, who will do all his business for him in return for commission on payments received. If he is finding a publisher for himself, he should first consider carefully the books which he reads, and those which he can look at in bookshops and libraries, besides getting what light he can on publishers from reviews of their books in the press, and advertisements and prospectuses. A wise author looks for a firm which issues books of the kind he has written, and designs and produces them attractively. He avoids publishers who advertise for manuscripts, which the better firms never do; they have no need. If he fails

A medieval artist's idea of two great ancient Greek philosophers, Plato and Socrates, the former of whom was also a great writer. This is not however a picture of writers at work, for Socrates seems to be neither reading nor writing but divining; by putting down his pen-knife at random he finds a word which is supposed to suggest an answer to a problem or prophesy a future event. Books were often used in this way in the middle ages

with one publisher he should try six to a dozen others before admitting defeat, because there are so many publishers looking for likely books, and their needs and opinions differ so widely. He must not send copies of his typescript to more than one publisher at a time, because this is very unfair to the publishers and would soon discredit him with them. He can feel confident that if his book is good of its own kind and has any chance of paying its way he can almost certainly find a publisher willing to risk his money on it.

Very few books are issued at the author's expense, and when they are, they are usually new poems by unknown writers or books so highly specialised that the sales are certain to be very small. Even these, however, if they are good enough, may sometimes be issued by publishers even though they expect to lose money on them, and nearly all other books are issued entirely at the risk and expense of the publishers, who make payments to the authors. These payments are nearly always by a royalty on sales, that is, a percentage of the selling price of every copy sold. This generally begins at 10 per cent on, say, the first three thousand copies sold, and then may rise as sales increase. (Percentages vary with the price and the kind of book.) So if sales are large the author as well as the publisher will benefit.

When a publisher has decided that he would like to publish the book he sends the author a contract containing many details about the book rights, serial rights, film rights, and all the other rights, and the author may wisely seek the advice of the Society of Authors before he signs it. In any case he should consider joining this Society, which exsits to look after authors' rights and interests.

There are many stories about authors making fortunes with their first books, and some of these stories are true. Yet a good many authors go on writing for years and even become well known without being more than poorly rewarded. When the Society of Authors conducted an enquiry in 1957 it found that—of the 607 authors who replied—73 per cent earned less than £1,000 a year from writing *of any kind*. Only 4 per cent earned more than £2,500 a year. A leading literary agent produced very similar figures independently, and said that while a few of the authors on his books earn up to £10,000, many who are "well known to the public, enjoy good critical acclaim and are generally well looked upon, earn less than £500 per annum".

It is difficult to earn a living by writing, and still more difficult to do so entirely by writing books, which few authors manage to do. Most of them, now as in the past, have to earn their living in some other way, and write when they can find time for it. Moreover, the public taste is so difficult to predict and can change so freakishly, that a well-known writer's books may suddenly stop selling, where-upon his income vanishes; or a writer who has long been unsuccessful may suddenly find his books selling in very large numbers. Fortunately for themselves very few authors write solely to make money.

Few are Chosen

Every working day hundreds of manuscripts arrive in British publishers' offices, and thousands more in those of other publishers all over the world. British publishers estimate that they accept two to three out of every hundred they receive, and since 20,000 new books (as well as 6,000 new editions of earlier books) are published in Britain every year, there must be many thousands of manuscripts always going the rounds. Sorting them out as they arrive is a heavy labour, but it must be done carefully. Some people think that an unknown author cannot get his work properly considered unless he can obtain a personal introduction to a publisher. This is nonsense. Publishers have to earn their living in a very difficult, highly competitive trade by finding books that sell, which means, if they are good publishers, good books that sell. So they cannot afford to miss the sort of books they want. If they do they go bankrupt.

The morning's pile in a publisher's editorial department falls into two classes, the expected and the unexpected. The first may include a new book by the firm's most famous author. If this is up to his usual standard, it will be greeted with enthusiasm. If it is not, it will probably have to be accepted all the same, because the publisher cannot risk losing him.

Other books may have been written on commission. Publishers often see a need for a particular kind of book on a particular subject and then persuade a suitably qualified author to write it. When it arrives, sometimes much later than the author promised, it may be excellent, and just what is needed; it may be a dull book; or it may be something quite different from what the author undertook to write. A great deal of tactful management may be required.

The unexpected manuscripts are the real excitement. No one who loves books, and most people in publishing do, can open a package containing manuscripts without something of a thrill. Has it arrived today—the masterpiece from an unknown author which everyone is looking for? Well, if the masterpiece is not there, after all, there are usually some strange arrivals to provoke curiosity.

A number have to be rejected after a very brief examination. If a publisher never issues novels, or law books, or school textbooks, for example, his editors will not waste time considering any of these, and obviously the authors should not have sent them to this particular firm. If the publisher has a life of Oliver Cromwell nearly ready for publication the offer of another, even if it is better, must be rejected. Other manuscripts can be seen, from reading a few pages of them, to be hopelessly bad or quite out of keeping with the firm's policy.

This weeding-out usually leaves a few manuscripts which need and receive very careful consideration. The publisher's editors may be able to "read" and report on some. Others will be sent to professional "readers" outside who are paid by the publisher. They may be literary critics (often writers themselves) or experts in anything from space research or the Elizabethan seamen to gardening. The reader's business is to say what kind of book it is, what its merits and defects are, and whether he thinks it likely to sell. If the first report is not decisive the manuscript has to go to a second reader. If he disagrees with the first it may have to go to a third. All this takes time and costs the publisher money. Finally there is, in most firms, an editorial meeting at which manuscripts, readers' reports and the Editorial Department's opinions are carefully considered, and it is then decided which manuscripts to accept, which to reject.

This process is slow, which makes it exasperating to the author, who may be kept waiting weeks for a decision, and it is troublesome and expensive for the publisher. But obviously it is all-important to both author and publisher, and must be done carefully.

The author whose work is acceptable will be sent a formal offer for it, and as

The devices, or colophons,

soon as a contract is signed the publisher will begin the highly complicated process of turning the manuscript into a book and then selling the book.

Designing Books

Every manufactured article you use has been designed by someone who had to decide its shape, colour and the materials of which it was to be made. Every printed carton, ticket, newspaper, poster and paper bag, and every book, has been similarly designed. You will soon notice if the book has been badly done—the type is too small, the headings do not stand out clearly, or the paper or binding is unpleasant in some way. But if it is well designed you may not notice it, because the type is easy to read and the whole style of the production is unobtrusive. It is simply a book, you think. But book design is by no means simple.

The first thing a book designer in a publisher's Production Department must do, when he receives a manuscript, is to find out what sort of book it is—dictionary, school book, novel, play, technical treatise on engineering, textbook of higher mathematics, picture book in colour, paperback or art book, to name a few possibilities. Obviously, these books should look very different from each other when they have been designed and printed; if, for example, the paperback and the art book got muddled up, there would be trouble! Next the designer finds out the probable number of copies to be printed and the approximate price. Then he will look through the manuscript (and illustrations, if there are any) with care, and decide what printing process and what printer are to be used. (Very few publishers are also printers.) The dictionary will go to a letterpress printer who is

used by some well-known publishers

very careful and accurate, since mistakes must not be made. The colour picture book may be printed by litho (lithography), and the paperback will be produced on a fast rotary machine which can both print and fold. The art book must be done by a printer capable of first-class illustration work, and may be reproduced by lithography or gravure. The designer has then to decide which of the numerous printing works which he knows is best equipped to do this particular job. (See pages 64–76 for descriptions of these processes.)

Next he settles the size of the page and the typeface to be used. Book sizes have names; Pott, Foolscap, Crown, Large Crown, Demy, Medium, Royal. The commonest size is an octavo (8vo), which means the size of the original hand-made paper when folded into eight—and since the paper sizes varied somewhat we have Demy 8vo ($8\frac{1}{2}''\times 5\frac{1}{2}''$) and Crown 8vo ($7\frac{1}{4}''\times 4\frac{7}{8}''$). This book which you are reading is Foolscap Quarto (4to), which means paper folded into four. Even bigger is Folio, where the paper is folded once.

There are very many different typefaces to choose from. Of course, the designer must use one which the printer has, but there will be a wide choice. Ever since the invention of printing new typefaces have been designed every decade or every year, and many of the oldest ones are still in use, like Bembo, in which this book is set. This is based closely on the typeface originally used in 1495 by Aldus Manutius, the great Venetian printer, in a book called *Petri Bembi de Aetna ad Angelum Chabrielem liber*. New typefaces are also popular, for instance Times New Roman, which Stanley Morison designed for *The Times* newspaper in 1931 and which is now widely used by all sorts of printers for all sorts of jobs. Some of them are fat and black—like this example:

This line is set in Plantin type

Others, although taking up the same space from the top to the bottom of the letters, are much lighter and more graceful, like this:

This line is set in Fournier type

Most typefaces consist of roman CAPITALS, SMALL CAPITALS, "lower case" (so called because it used to be kept in the lower of the two cases or trays full of type at which the compositor worked), *ITALIC CAPITALS* and *italic lower case* and arabic figures 1 2 3 4, etc. Some typefaces have italic figures *1 2 3 4*, etc., and a **Bold** version as well.

This line is set in Bembo Bold type

All these can be skilfully and unobtrusively used in books to help the reader find the chapter or part of a chapter he wants.

Besides these "text" types there are rather more exciting "display" types which are used for jackets, title pages, advertisements, etc. Here are a few of them:

ALBERTUS

GROTESQUE

CASTELLAR

STUDIO

UNION PEARL

IMPERIAL SCRIPT

Using some of these is great fun.

If a book is long, then a fairly narrow type must be used so that as many words as possible can be fitted into a page. If it has light pencil illustrations the type must be light, too, otherwise it will make the illustrations look weak. Shiny art paper makes types look lighter, so on this a blackish type is necessary.

The designer tells the printer the typeface and size to be used, how long the lines shall be and how much space is to be left between them. (This spacing is called "leading" and is calculated to a one hundred and forty-fourth of an inch.) He gives details of the style and sizes of chapter titles, headings, etc. In a well-designed book the paper, the size and shape of the page, the various widths of the margins, the size and style of the page headings and chapter headings, the design and size of the type, the length of the line and the space, if any, between the lines, are all nicely adjusted to each other, to make the page easy to read, unobtrusively pleasant to look at, and suitable to the subject-matter. But book designers, like all craftsmen, are sometimes cramped by limitations of cost and materials.

Given all the details the printer makes "specimen pages", showing some parts of the manuscript set up in the style specified, so that the designer can see what the printed book will look like. The printer also works out how many pages long the book will be and how much he will charge for printing it.

The publisher can then work out what the selling price of the book must be. He adds up all the "production costs"—printing, illustrations, paper, blocks, jackets and binding—for the number of copies he will want to print. This may be anything between one thousand and fifty thousand or in rare cases several hundred thousand. Then he divides the total by the number of copies to find out the cost per copy. To this he adds allowances for advertising, overheads (the rent of his offices, wages of his staff and cost of sending books to booksellers, etc.), payments to the author, and the firm's profit. This total gives the "trade" price, at which the book will be sold to the bookseller, which is usually about two-thirds of the published price. The difference between the two goes to the bookseller, who has to pay all his own overheads from it, and they are heavy.

When the number to be printed and the price to be charged have been finally settled, the publisher's Production Department can get on with the job of organising the manufacture of the book.

First of all the designer will look critically at the printer's specimen page and mark any changes which are necessary. Then he will do the "layout" for the "prelims". This is short for preliminary pages—the title page, dedication, contents, list of illustrations, acknowledgments, and foreword—all those things which come before the text proper. A "layout" is a careful drawing of each page showing the printer what sizes of type to use and where to place the words on the page. It is important that the prelims should be well laid out so that the reader can easily find what he wants. The title page is often difficult to design. Next time you are in a library look at the title pages of several books and try to decide whether they are well designed or not and why.

The completed layout is sent to the printer with the marked specimen page, the manuscript and an order asking him to set up the type and telling him what proofs to supply. Several sets of galley proofs may be needed, proofs on long slips of paper with the type in long, continuous columns. (See page 66 below.) These proofs have to be read by the publisher's Editorial Department and sent to the author, who also reads them, to correct printer's errors. Sometimes the author makes alterations also, and these are so expensive—since every letter in the type has to be changed separately by hand—that he may have to pay part of the cost.

Using the corrected galleys, the printer makes up the type into pages, and then sends page proofs to the publisher, who may need as many as a hundred and fifty sets, one to be passed by the author, others to be used in the publisher's offices and the rest to go to the publisher's travellers and to booksellers and perhaps reviewers.

The publisher always wants to know in advance when these will be ready, and the Production Department will try to work out months beforehand when the book can be published, so that everybody will be ready for it—the Advertising Department, the Sales Department, the warehouse, and the travellers who show the book to the booksellers. It is not always possible to keep to these dates, because so many people are involved, but they are often given well in advance.

While the printer is setting up the type the artist and blockmaker are getting on with the illustrations, if there are any, so that the blocks will be ready to put into the proofs. The paper will be chosen and ordered (it is often specially made for the book) and the binder will make up a "dummy copy" exactly the same size and thickness as the finished book.

This enables the Production Department (or sometimes the Publicity Department) to get on with the book jacket, and nowadays this is very important, for if it is good it catches the customer's eye and makes him pick up the book and look inside, so it must be the kind of jacket which will attract people likely to buy that particular book. A lurid jacket would kill the sale of a scholarly work. A dull jacket would be equally bad for a humorous novel. Whether the jacket is to be simply lettered or to bear a picture, the artist must be carefully chosen. The Production Department sends him a copy of the manuscript, with details of the sort of design which is needed and the number of colours to be used. The artist does one or more "roughs"—coloured sketches of his ideas—and the Production Department chooses one and asks the artist to send the finished drawing quickly. (A few firms have all their jackets designed in their own offices. Different publishing firms have different methods in this as in almost everything else.) The jacket is needed long before the book is ready to be published, so that the travellers have time to show it to the booksellers beforehand.

After the page proofs have been read, and the index—if there is one—made and proofed, the book can "go to press"—that is, be printed off. The binder will have to be told what binding style to use and supplied with the "brass" block for the lettering, and he will bind up as many copies of the book as the publisher needs. It is not usual to bind up all the copies printed, unless the publisher is sure he will sell the book quickly, because this might be a waste of money.

The time taken to produce a book varies enormously, but eight or nine months is a fair average from the printer's receipt of the manuscript to publication day.

Making Books

The paper on which books are printed comes from a paper mill. A modern paper-making machine is very large indeed, sometimes as much as a hundred and fifty feet long. At one end is a tank containing a pulp of wood, or a mixture of esparto grass and wood. The impurities are removed from the pulp, for otherwise flaws would appear in the finished paper. The pulp flows on to a moving belt of wire mesh which shakes out some of the water and mixes the fibres so that they lie criss-crossed in all directions. More water is removed when the paper passes over suction boxes and then between rollers. The paper is by this time fairly firm and is carried by absorbent felt between more rollers which squeeze out more water. Heated steel cylinders then dry the paper and cold steel rollers give it a good smooth surface. Finally it is wound on to a huge reel in a continuous strip. A newspaper press will print the paper direct from the reel and cut it into sheets afterwards. If the paper is intended for books, however, it must first be divided into narrower rolls or cut into sheets. The Fourdrinier machine can make anything from 200 to 1,000 feet of paper in a minute, in rolls up to 20 feet wide.

To see how the blank sheets of paper are turned into books we must visit a printing works. Here we shall see, first of all, the composing machines, usually Monotype. The operator taps out the words to be printed (the *copy* as he calls it) on a keyboard which looks similar to a typewriter, but has 306 keys—seven

An early Fourdrinier papermaking machine

alphabets, giving capitals, small capitals, "lower-case" (small) letters, italics, etc., besides figures and spaces. It is not as complicated as it sounds, and a skilful operator works very quickly. The machine measures the width of every letter and counts the number of spaces between words. When the operator nears the end of a line a bell rings and the machine measures the blank space left, divides this by the number of spaces and shows on a drum how much additional space has to be put in after each word in order to bring the last word to the right-hand margin. This is called *justification*, and it is this which gives a page of type a straight margin on the right-hand side as well as on the left.

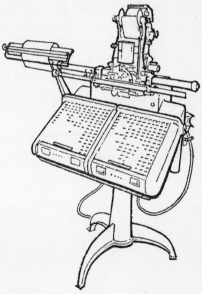

The keyboard does not produce type-written sheets; it punches holes in a long roll of paper. The holes represent letters, punctuation marks or spaces, according to their position on the paper. When it is finished this roll is put on a second

The Monotype keyboard, with the "copy" on the left and, above, the roll of paper which is punched with holes representing letters, punctuation marks etc.

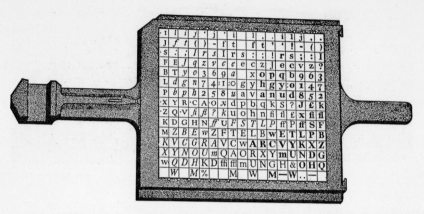

The matrix case, in which the printing surface of the piece of type is moulded

machine which makes the type. Compressed air blows through holes in the roll of paper moving a case containing matrices for all the letters of the alphabet so that the right letter comes into position over a type-mould. Molten metal is pumped into the mould, which is cooled immediately by a stream of water. The matrix case then moves into position for the next letter and the finished type slips into line in a galley. (The galley is a steel tray which holds the type until it is divided up into pages.)

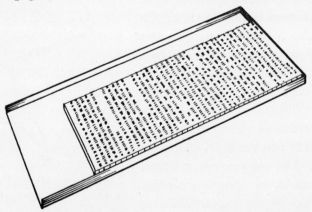

The galley which holds the type until it is divided into pages

Now the galley goes to the compositor, who has it read to make sure that everything is correct, and alters by hand any mistakes that have crept in. The type in the galley reads mirrorwise so that it will be the right way round when it is printed, but an experienced compositor can read it as quickly as you read a page of ordinary print. A *proof* (a trial printing) is pulled at this stage. It is called a galley proof and it enables corrections and alterations to be made before the type is divided up into pages. Galley proofs may then go to the publisher, and from him to the author, for checking. When they are returned the compositor makes the corrections and if there are illustrations to go in with the type he puts these into their places. He then divides the type into pages, putting in the page numbers and the headlines at the top of every page, and ties up each page with cord to hold it together for the time being. A number of pages, usually thirty-two or sixty-four, are printed at once, so the compositor arranges the pages of type in the right order on a table top of smooth steel, and places pieces of metal between them to make the margins. Then he clamps the whole thing tightly together in a steel frame. The frame with the type in it is called a *forme*. Page proofs are taken from the forme, and are sent to the printer's reader, publisher and possibly the author, who make any corrections necessary—although corrections are very expensive when the type is in page. (Sometimes the publisher gets page proofs only, sometimes galley and page proofs.) Then the forme is locked up and the type is ready for the press.

The machine and the type have next to be made ready for printing, and in particular when the type has been laid on the flat steel bed of the printing press it has to be very delicately adjusted so that it will print evenly. If this is not done some parts of a type page will be black and some grey. This *make-ready* is one of the stages in the printing process at which craftsmanship counts a great deal— and a good craftsman can get much better results than an inferior one from the same machine and materials.

Once the machine has been started it will go on turning out printed sheets, and counting them, until someone stops it. (The machine can turn itself off if something goes wrong. Usually, however, someone watches it to make sure that all the sheets are well printed.) A feeder slides sheets of paper into the press one by one from a pile at the end. The forme of type on its steel bed moves to

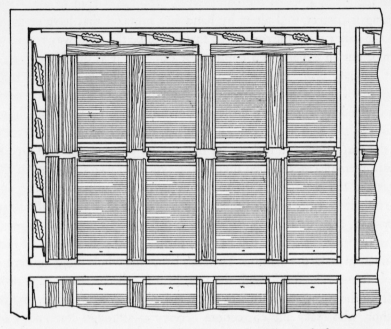

The forme – showing the pages of type clamped together ready for printing

and fro under rollers which take up ink from an ink-slab and spread it evenly on the type. The forme passes under a cylinder carrying a sheet of paper which is pressed against the type, and then on to the growing pile of printed sheets. The machine takes in another blank sheet, repeating the whole process until the required number of copies has been made.

The press just described prints one side of the paper only, and so all the sheets have to be run through a second time to print the other side. There are more complicated machines which can print both sides of the paper, one immediately after the other, and yet another kind can print in two or more colours. All these are various types of flat-bed cylinder machines.

A duplicate can be made of a page of type by covering it with *flong,* papier-maché, which is put under a heavy press. When removed it provides a mould in which a cast of the type (known as a stereo plate, or stereo) can be made from

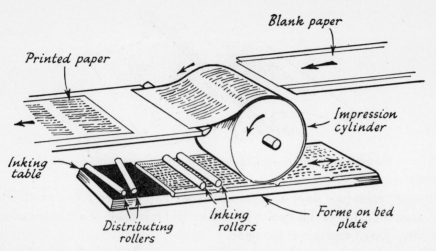

Blank paper

Printed paper

Impression cylinder

Inking table

Distributing rollers

Inking rollers

Forme on bed plate

This diagram shows how a flat-bed cylinder machine works. The paper is gripped on the impression cylinder and printed when the forme moves under the cylinder

molten metal, plastic, rubber, nylon or some other material. Stereos can be used for printing, to save wear on the original type, and they can be curved for use on a rotary printing press. This is much faster than a flat-bed machine and is therefore generally used for printing cheap books, newspapers or periodicals in large numbers.

When the press has done its work we have a pile of large sheets of paper each printed with thirty-two, sixty-four or even more pages. The next stage is the folding machine. As each sheet of paper is fed into the machine it is centred under a knife which descends on it, pushing it between two rollers and so folding it down the middle.

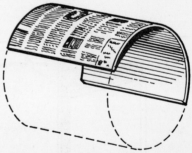

The curved stereo plate used in a rotary machine (only half is indicated by dotted lines)

The sheet is then carried on to a second set of knife and rollers which folds it again, and the process is repeated until the sheet is folded to page size. This makes the sheets into *signatures,* or sections folded down the middle, each of sixteen or

The knife and rollers which fold the large sheets into page-sized signatures

thirty-two pages (one sheet of paper may make two or even four signatures). If you look at the top of this book you will see that it is made of a number of such signatures joined together at the spine.

If there are to be any illustrations printed separately from the text these are wrapped round the signatures or inserted into them. Sometimes single illustrations are pasted in. At this stage, too, the endpapers are pasted on to the first and last signatures.

Next the signatures have to go to the collating machine to be put into the right order to make the finished book. A moving conveyor belt passes under a box which contains a pile of copies of the first signature of the book. One copy drops face downwards on to the belt which then moves on to the next box, where a copy of the second signature drops on top of the first. The belt moves on, collecting a copy of each signature as it goes, until finally all the signatures are collated and the book is complete. The sewing machine then sews through the centre of each section and joins them together securely. Some books are sewn on to tapes, which you can see under the endpaper on the front and back boards of many books.

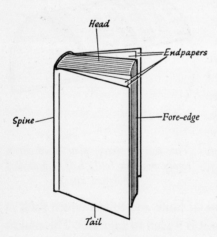

The parts of the book

The book is now pressed, which is called *nipping* in the trade, and the edges are trimmed smooth by a machine gruesomely called a guillotine, which consists of three very sharp knives. The book is gripped in a clamp and the first knife descends, cutting the fore-edge. Then two more at right-angles to the first trim the head- and tail-edges.

If you look carefully at any thickish bound book you will see that only the top and bottom are exactly square; the spine is gently rounded and the fore-edge curves inwards to correspond. This is done to make the book open more easily. The machine which does it is called the rounding and backing machine. When this has done its job our book begins to be recognisable as a book, but, of course, it has no cover yet.

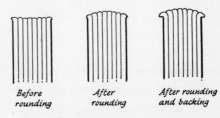

Before rounding   After rounding   After rounding and backing

The effect of rounding and backing

Today many books, particularly paper-backs, are not sewn together in sections at all. Instead all the edges, including the back, are cut flush, leaving the book as a pile of separate pages. A plastic solution is brushed into the back edge, which, when it has dried, holds the pages together just as firmly as in a sewn book, when properly done. Unsewn binding is much simpler than the traditional type of binding, but it has certain disadvantages, for it cannot be used with some kinds of paper, and books made in this way cannot easily be rebound when they become worn.

The case, a hard cover, is made separately on a machine which places two boards (rectangles of cardboard), one for the front cover and one for the back, in position on a piece of glued material cut to the right size. A strip of paper is placed between the boards to stiffen the spine. Then the edges of the material, which may be cloth or paper, or some synthetic fabric, are folded over the board and stuck down.

The case then goes to a blocking press, where the title of the book and the author's name are stamped on. The letters have been cut out on a block of brass which is heated and stamped on to the spine, leaving a permanent impression of the letters. If no colour is used the blocking is said to be *blind*. If colour, or gold or silver is wanted, a foil, that is a ribbon of thin paper or cellophane holding

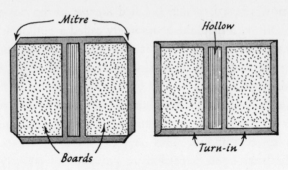

Making a case

powdered colour or metal, passes between the case and the heated block, and the colour is transferred from the foil to the spine of the case. Coloured ink can also be used, without heating the brass.

Meanwhile the book is prepared for its case on the lining machine. First the spine is given a coat of glue and a piece of coarse cloth called mull is pressed on to it. Then sometimes more glue is rolled on to the spine and a strip of paper is stuck on top of the mull.

Finally the book and its case are joined together by the casing machine. Here the endpapers receive a coating of paste and the case is placed in position and pressed down on to the book, which now goes to be pressed to make it quite firm. If it is to have a dust-jacket this must be wrapped round it by hand. Then, at last, the book is ready to be packed up and delivered to the publisher's warehouse, ready to be sent to the bookshop.

There are many different ways of printing illustrations for a book, and some of the processes are very complicated indeed, much too complicated to be explained fully here. The method of printing described earlier in the chapter is called letterpress, and some kinds of illustrations, half-tones, wood engravings and line blocks, are also printed by letterpress. Because they can be printed at the same time as the text, line blocks and wood engravings are cheap to reproduce.

A line block is made by photographing a drawing and exposing the negative on to a sheet of zinc or magnesium. Then the zinc is treated so that the drawing is protected and the whole sheet is immersed in a bath of acid which eats away the unprotected metal. This process is called etching. When the zinc sheet is taken out of the acid the drawing is left standing up in relief.

A line block can reproduce illustrations in black and white, but it cannot give intermediate shades of grey as well. Photographs and lithographs both contain intermediate shades and so must be produced by some other means.

Photographs are most often printed as half-tone plates. When making the block the original photograph has to be photographed again, using a half-tone screen in front of the photographic plate in the camera. This screen consists of a sheet of glass, engraved with two sets of parallel lines at right-angles, which has the effect of breaking the picture up into a series of tiny dots. If you look closely at a photograph in a newspaper you can actually see the dots which make up the picture, large where the picture is to appear dark, and small in the lighter patches. The screen used for photographs in most newspapers is coarse, only sixty-five lines to the inch, but in book illustrations a finer screen is used, and it is very difficult to see the separate dots without the help of a magnifying-glass. The half-tone block is made by printing the negative, photographed through the screen, on to a sheet of copper, and etching it with acid just like a line block. As you can imagine, a great deal of skill is needed to make a good negative and to etch the block properly.

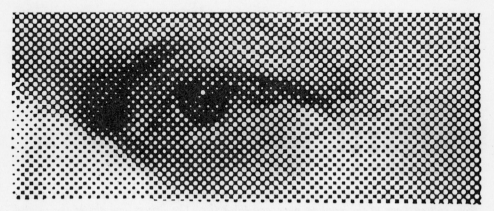

Part of a half-tone photograph, much enlarged. You can see what it represents by holding it away from you

Coloured photographs can also be printed by the half-tone process, but four different plates have to be made, one to print each of the three primary colours, red, blue and yellow, and one for black. Colour filters are used in the camera with the half-tone screen to make the four plates which are etched in the normal way. The paper has to go through the printing press four times, once for each colour. The finished picture is made up of countless tiny dots in the four colours which together give the impression not only of the primary colours but of all the other colours as well.

A disadvantage of letterpress half-tone is that for good results shiny-coated paper has to be used, so the illustrations have to be printed separately from the text unless this, too, is printed on the shiny paper.

Photogravure plates, on the other hand, can be printed on matt paper, but they are very expensive to make, so they are only economical when a large number of copies is to be printed. In the photogravure process the picture is once again broken up into a series of dots by using a screen in the camera. This time, however, the dots do not stand up from the surface of the printing plate, but are hollowed out of it in minute cavities of varying depth. The deeper cavities hold more ink and so print darker than the shallow ones. By using colour filters and four printings photogravure can reproduce colour photographs as well. In fact, colour photo-

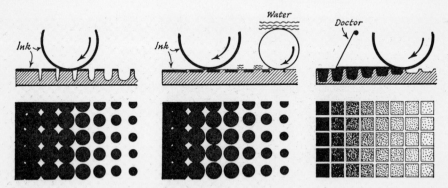

The principles of letterpress half-tone, lithography and photogravure. The top row of diagrams show cross-sections of the printing plate and ink-roller. The bottom row shows the printed results much enlarged. (The doctor is a blade which removes surplus ink from a photogravure plate)

gravure has a quality of depth and brilliance which cannot be obtained in colour half-tones.

For lithography, as you can see from the sketch above, the printing surface is flat. It is divided into printing and non-printing parts by an application of the principle that grease and water will not mix. If a picture is drawn on certain kinds of stone with a greasy crayon and then flooded with water only the greasy part, the drawing, will absorb printing ink, which is greasy too. So, by pressing a sheet of paper on to the stone's surface, the drawing can be printed. Specially treated metal plates can be used in the same way. In this process the artist himself may prepare the printing surface, so reproducing his original idea more directly than by any other.

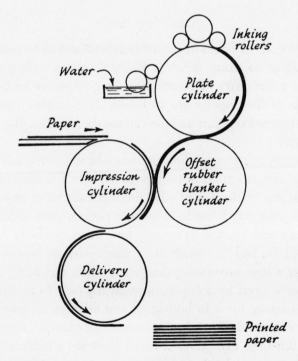

A diagram explaining offset printing. Ink is transferred from the type on the plate cylinder to the rubber roller, and from the roller to the paper on the impression cylinder

Lithography can also be used to reproduce photographs or line drawings. As with letterpress half-tone and photogravure a screen must be used in the camera when tones intermediate between black and white are wanted. Very often lithographic illustrations are not printed directly on to the paper, but are first "offset" on to a cylinder covered with rubber. A film of ink is transferred from the lithographic plate to the rubber, which then rolls the ink on to the paper. As the rubber presses gently but very firmly against the plate, and again on the paper, every small detail of the picture is clearly printed.

It is possible to print a whole book by photo-lithography, text and illustrations as well. This method is often used for reprinting books when the printer no longer has the original type, for it saves the trouble and expense of resetting the text.

Marketing Books

Writing or talking about books in general is difficult and all too easily misleading, because they are of so many different kinds. A school arithmetic textbook, a detective story, a dictionary of biochemistry, a guide-book to London and the complete works of Shakespeare are all books. That is, they consist of printed sheets of paper fastened together and they all use the alphabet. But what else have they in common?

This is the publisher's greatest difficulty when he sets out to sell his books. The maker of motor cars, stockings or toothpaste has very few different items to sell, and to advertise one of them is to advertise them all. More important still, the sales of any one item may bring in thousands, perhaps even millions, of pounds. But almost every new book is an entirely new thing, publicity for it may have nothing to build on, and the maximum possible sales are nearly always far too small to pay for a large advertising campaign, which nowadays costs thousands of pounds. A new novel by a famous novelist has only to be announced to set hosts of readers asking for it in bookshops and libraries. A new issue of Who's Who, or a new volume of The Arden Shakespeare, for example, is sure to command a certain sale. But these exceptions are few. How are a publisher's sales staff to persuade people to buy a book which has no such automatic appeal? There are too many books chasing too few readers.

A new book is announced, with a descriptive note usually called a "blurb", in the firm's list of forthcoming books, and this is posted to hundreds or even thousands of booksellers, librarians and individual readers who have asked for the publisher's lists, at home and overseas.

For a book of some special importance a separate prospectus may be printed, with two, four or more pages describing the work and its author, perhaps giving a specimen page or a specimen illustration. Booksellers take copies of this to give to their customers, and there may be a special distribution; e.g. a prospectus of an important new medical book may be posted to every doctor in Britain and to many overseas. But this is expensive, and cannot be done for many books.

The publisher's representatives, who are constantly travelling about Britain, will show copies of the book, or proofs of it, or at least the wrapper, to as many bookshops (or schools) as possible in the month or so before publication, to collect orders. This is called "subscribing" and nothing is more important to sales, for if many bookshops display a book it is brought to the notice of large numbers of possible buyers. This is particularly valuable, if not essential, in the case of paperbacks.

Three or four weeks before publication review copies are sent out (free) to suitable newspapers and periodicals—a large number of copies of a book which may secure a large general public, a few copies only, to specialist periodicals, of, say, a technical book on nuclear engineering. Many of these copies will never be reviewed. Favourable reviews of a specialised book or textbook by authorities on its subject can certainly lead to sales. But a "general" book, a novel, biography or travel book, for example, may have numerous reviews, all of them favourable and yet be a complete failure so far as sales go, while in other cases an enthusiastic review seems to give a book a splendid start. Radio and television notices have similarly mixed results. Not enough books are reviewed to satisfy readers, authors or publishers, because there is not enough space in the press. Reviews vary much in quality, partly because reviewers are often badly paid. Some air their own opinions of the subject and show no signs of having read a single page of the book. Others are honest, illuminating, and helpful to the reader by giving him a clear idea of the book's subject-matter, merits and defects. But an intelligent reader can soon learn to distinguish between the good and the bad reviews.

Finally there are press advertisements, very expensive and often frustrating to the publisher's publicity manager because the potential profits on a book are very rarely large enough for him to make a splash. It is an old saying, partly true, that publishers advertise their books simply to please their authors and to attract other authors.

If it plese ony man spirituel or temporel to bye ony pyes of two and thre comemoracios of salisburi vse enpryntid after the forme of this preset lettre whiche ben wel and truly correct, late hym come to westmonester in to the almonesrye at the reed pale and he shal haue them good chepe .·.

Supplico stet cedula

A fifteenth century advertisement. A poster issued by William Caxton, the first English printer, advertising a church service book. (See page 37)

Everyone agrees that there is one thing certain to bring sales: enthusiastic recommendation from one reader to another, but not even the most expert publisher can say for certain whether any particular book will be given this passport to popularity.

The great consolation is that any reader who wants to find out about new books or old, of any kind, can do so by the methods explained on pages 88–91 below.

When the binder has delivered the copies of the book to the publisher it is ready to be launched on the world.

Every publisher has to maintain a warehouse—or a part of one if he shares it with other firms—to store his books. For a small firm there may be few difficulties in this, for a large one there are many. One of the famous firms has over 17,000 "titles" (different books) in stock. One of the famous paperback firms takes in and despatches over fifteen million books every year. The stock of a particular book may be three copies one day and 3,000 or 300,000 copies the next day. The books may occupy several miles of shelving. Orders come in from retail and wholesale booksellers all over Britain and all over the world. An order may be for one copy of one title or 15,000 copies of one title; or it may be for 1,100 titles, the number for each varying from one copy to several thousands. The books for each order have to be collected from the shelves, and checked against the order, the invoice and address label have to be typed, and the books have to be packed, weighed and despatched, sometimes accompanied by a number of complicated documents if they are going overseas.

One day, perhaps, someone will invent an electronic device, efficient and not too expensive, which selects and assembles the books in their separate groups by an entirely automatic process. Meanwhile all big firms have partly mechanised systems, and the rest of the work is done, as it has been for centuries, by men and women "looking out" the books. There are mistakes and delays sometimes, and a bookseller who gets the wrong books is naturally furious, but on the whole the distributive systems seem to work quite well. They could be made to work better by spending more money on them, but to find the money the prices of books would have to be raised very considerably, and publishers are always struggling to keep them down—largely from fear that sales would suffer. As it is, prices go up every time the cost of printing and paper rises. The prices of many other things have, however, risen more.

The number of copies of books to be handled continues to increase. The figures below show how British publishers' sales (at trade prices) have grown since 1937, the first year in which the statistics were collected:

Year	Total sales £	U.K. £	Export £	Export percentage
1937	10,507,204	7,361,047	3,146,157	30
1953	44,892,291	29,325,417	15,566,874	34.7
1963	90,142,709	51,098,858	39,043,851	43.1

The U.K. sales are depressing. (The amount spent on gambling in the U.K. during 1962 has been estimated at more than £850,000,000.) But the increase in export sales is promising, and it is far from being due entirely to the higher prices of books. The latest figures include millions of cheap paperbacks and textbooks. In Britain, and in most other countries, especially the developing countries of Asia and Africa, there is a rapidly growing demand for education to meet the needs of life today. Millions of people now realise that books (and periodicals) are essential to education. The demand overseas for British publications of all kinds is due to the adoption of English as the world language, and to the quality of English literature, creative and technical, and the enterprise of British publishers. Many books now published in Britain have been specially written for countries in Asia and Africa, some of them in the local languages. But there is rapidly growing competition from books and periodicals published in English in U.S.A., Russia, China and many other countries, and these are often subsidised by their governments.

We in Britain must export or starve, since it is only by our exports that we can buy the great quantities of imported food which we need, so all our exports are obviously very important. But this is specially true of our books and periodicals, because they lead overseas readers to buy more of our goods and because they spread British ideas.

Fortunately British publishers now get some help overseas from the Government through the British Council and the Central Office of Information, but it is still far too small.

The growing demand all over the world for books of all kinds in all languages is an encouraging picture, not only for the people who write or sell books, but for society at large.

The Bookseller's Role

Good bookshops are fascinating places to anyone with any interest in books, but nowadays they are much more than that. They are essential to any community if it is to be educated and progressive. There are not yet nearly enough good bookshops in Britain, largely because the profits are so hard earned and the book-buying public is so small. Few bookshops in Britain can make a living by selling new books alone. Most of them have to sell stationery and other things as well. In Britain the bookseller's greatest problem is this: there are about 200,000 books in print here, and about 26,000 new books and new editions are issued every year. The bookseller has to decide which of all those books to keep in stock and obviously he can stock only a small percentage of the total. He has to pay for most of them, whether he sells them or not, so he must prophesy his customers' needs and tastes with a high degree of accuracy if he is not to lose money and go out of business.

The second great problem is that any customer may want any one of those thousands of books. If it is in stock there is no difficulty, and should he decide to buy it after looking at it he and the bookseller will be happy. If the book is not in stock it can be ordered, and the ordering is easy enough if the customer has the author and title right. It is easier still if he knows the publisher as well. Often this is not difficult. Author, title and publisher are given on every title page, and in all the reviews, advertisements and prospectuses. But if he knows neither author nor publisher and has got the title half wrong, the bookseller has to bring all his skill and knowledge to bear, and use his reference books ingeniously.

When a foreign customer asked for *Big Hopes*, and didn't know the author, it took the bookseller a few minutes to divine that this was Charles Dickens' novel *Great Expectations*. Many requests are even more difficult than that. Once in a while there is a teaser such as:

"Can you get me a book that was published in Russian in Czechoslovakia six years ago?" (That can probably be done if the book is still in print.)

Far more often the difficult enquiry is very vague. "I want a book about a fish which was reviewed in one of the Sunday papers about two years ago. All I can remember is that it was a very clever fish." (Well, there was a book about a dolphin, and dolphins are remarkably intelligent. Not strictly fish; marine mammals; but near enough. Let's see where that clue leads.)

"Is there a good Italian cookery book?" (That's easy; there are several.)

"Which is the most authoritative, up-to-date book on the archaeology of Sumer?" (Not quite so easy, perhaps.)

"Can you recommend a book on flying models of aeroplanes?" (Again, there are several.)

"I want a nice book for my niece in Edinburgh. She's about fifteen, but I don't really know what sort of book she likes." (The best answer to that may be to sell uncle a Book Token, which the girl can exchange in her nearest bookshop, for books of her own choosing.)

At the end of the day the bookseller may find he has fifty or a hundred orders for books issued by nearly as many publishers. A large bookshop may have many more than that at busy times. Some of these orders go direct to publishers with whom the bookseller does a good deal of business. The rest of the orders go to a wholesaler. Some of the books will be reprinting or binding, some perhaps permanently out of print, but the majority will arrive within three weeks at most, and some much more quickly.

Unfortunately there are very few large bookshops outside university towns. But all good booksellers are booklovers. (If they weren't they would leave the book trade for something more profitable.) They take more than a commercial pleasure in helping a customer to find just the book he or she needs. They are glad to give information and guidance, and they do not press people to buy, so no one need hesitate to wander into a bookshop to look round. There are books which are interesting and useful to anyone who can read. (It isn't fair to try to read a book right through in the shop!) It is a very satisfactory thing to look at a book carefully before deciding to buy it.

Libraries for All

Today almost everyone in England has a public library within easy reach. When you go into your library you probably find a reading-room with shelves full of books where you can browse as you please. When you have found a book which looks interesting you can take it home to read at leisure. If, on the other hand, you cannot find the one you want, you can ask the librarian to help you. If it is not there, it may even be borrowed from another library for you. You pay nothing when you borrow books, since all these services are provided by the town or county council from the local rates, to which everyone contributes directly or indirectly.

Many facilities are offered by a large town library, the most important being, of course, the lending of books. Everyone who lives in the town may borrow books with the minimum of formality. There are usually separate reading-rooms for children and adults, so that they can more easily find the sort of books they like.

A very important part of any library is the reference section, where you can consult books on all subjects as well as general reference books such as encyclopaedias, dictionaries and atlases. The librarian is skilled in finding information on any subject, for he is expected to answer all kinds of enquiries: "I want a list of all the Archbishops of Canterbury." "How can I cure fish of tapeworm?" "Where can I find out about the Incas of Peru?" "Do you know of any amateur acting groups in this district?" These are typical of the questions which may be fired at the omniscient reference librarian. He may be asked to produce anything from a coloured picture of a peacock to a street map of Chipping Ongar or an illustration showing the costume worn by a Tibetan lama.

Many libraries now make a point of collecting and preserving material about local history. This collection may contain old photographs, newspaper cuttings, maps, posters and theatre programmes as well as books and pamphlets. Particularly valuable is the file of the local newspaper, which may cover many years. From this you can find out what was happening in your town ten, twenty or even fifty or a hundred years ago.

In addition the library often acts as an information centre about current activities and usually displays a notice board covered with announcements of local events, details of club meetings, programmes of evening classes, lectures and other similar activities. There may be discussions, lectures, film shows and gramophone recitals taking place in the library itself.

It has recently become possible to borrow music scores, gramophone records and pictures from some of the larger libraries, and it is probable that more and more of them will be able to provide these extra facilities in the future.

In small towns and villages, however, the library must be less ambitious, for it is working on a smaller budget. It may be open only on two or three days in the week. Indeed, in very small villages it is not practicable to have a permanent library building at all, and so a large van—a "mobile library"—is used to take books to country areas. The van travels round a large district, stopping at selected places on the route for perhaps half an hour before going on to the next place.

As soon as it arrives the villagers flock to return their books and choose new ones to last until the next visit, perhaps a week or even a fortnight later. In winter bad weather may prevent the van from going on its rounds, particularly in the mountainous parts of Scotland and Wales, and it may be quite impossible to say when the van will arrive.

Although the number of books which a van can carry at one time is limited to about 2,000 volumes, which are changed regularly, they usually include a fair selection of new and popular books. If any borrower wants a particular book which is not on the shelves the librarian will bring it on his next round, or at least as soon as he can obtain it. So, if you live in a country area far from any of the larger libraries, you may have to wait before getting the book which you want, but you can actually borrow any book which is available from the best city libraries or, indeed, from any library in Britain. Sometimes, if a book is urgently needed by a student and it is not in any British library it may be sent from a library abroad, from Warsaw, perhaps, or Washington.

Britain is well provided with library services, for it is a small country and communications are easy. Our public library system has been growing for over a hundred years and it is now highly developed. Not all countries are so fortunate. Where conditions are bad there are enormous difficulties to be overcome in providing even a skeleton library service. In Africa, for example, there are large areas with no proper roads and boxes of books may be taken to remote villages by aeroplane, but many places can get no books at all. Even in countries like U.S.A. and Australia many people live far from the nearest town and it may well be a hundred miles or more from one town to the next. Where it is possible these areas are served by library vans which cover hundreds of miles, but they cannot visit all the isolated farms. Books are sometimes sent by post, but this is a very unsatisfactory method.

There are many other problems. In tropical countries all kinds of precautions must be taken to prevent books from being attacked by mildew and damp or being eaten by insects. Countries where books are rare may be obliged to provide reference libraries only, since a book taken away from the library might never be seen again. In other countries the public are not allowed to handle the books unsupervised, and have to ask the librarian for any book they want.

Although it will never be possible to serve widely scattered communities as efficiently as the compact, highly populated areas, all these difficulties are gradually being overcome. Library services are developing all over the world. The British Council maintains lending and reference libraries in more than seventy countries overseas, helping to make British publications available everywhere.

Public libraries are not the only lending libraries in Britain, of course. There are also subscription libraries run by some bookshops and large stores. They provide the latest and most popular books and they give their readers special services which cannot be given by a public library. Members pay a subscription, which is usually higher if they want to borrow the very latest books.

A small commercial library may be run as a sideline to a sweet shop or stationers. Here you pay a few pence a week for every book that you borrow. The books stocked are usually popular novels: detective stories, "westerns", "romances", and other light fiction.

Six great libraries are entitled to a copy of every book which is published in the United Kingdom. These deposit libraries, as they are called, are the British Museum, the Bodleian Library at Oxford, the Cambridge University Library, the National Library of Scotland, the National Library of Wales and the Library of Trinity College, Dublin.

University and school libraries stock the books which are required by the students. Newspaper libraries consist largely of files of newspaper cuttings indexed and arranged so that any piece of information required for an article in tomorrow's paper can be traced in an instant. Government departments, large firms and research establishments all have libraries to provide books and periodicals needed by the staff for their work. Specialists must read widely about the latest developments in their subject; research workers must be informed about the work other people are doing in the same field; scientists must know what has already been discovered before proceeding to their own discoveries. The material needed by all these people can be supplied by libraries which accumulate and organise highly specialised information on their subjects.

So as well as providing books for the entertainment and information of the general public the library is also a sort of store-cupboard of knowledge which can be drawn on by the specialists who will contribute to the discoveries of the future. It is therefore very important that everyone should be able to find the book or the information that he needs; that is why every good librarian makes it his aim to "bring the right book to the right person at the right time".

The Paperback Revolution

Books with paper covers are by no means new. After printing began in Europe books with soft covers appeared in many countries. One of the oldest known, printed in 1494, is in the British Museum. In some countries they remained popular. In France, for example, nearly all books are still published in paper covers, and the book buyer or librarian who wants to keep a book permanently has it bound for him in the style he likes. But French publishers are now issuing more books in hard covers.

In Britain, however, the great majority of books have long been published in hard covers. Cheap paperback series were by no means unknown in the nineteenth and early twentieth centuries, but they were always of limited appeal and minor importance.

What *is* new today is the tremendous world-wide popularity of cheap paperbacks. This is what is called the "paperback revolution", for it is indeed a revolutionary change in book buying and publishing. The pioneer was Sir Allen Lane, who founded Penguin Books Ltd. in 1935 and has been their presiding genius ever since. So many previous attempts had failed that no one in the British book trade expected him to succeed, but he has succeeded so well that (although few readers notice publishers' names, which is a great pity) "Penguins" are now world-famous.

Until after the war Penguins had almost a monopoly in Britain. Then other series of similar size and price began to appear, and in the last few years the stream of paperbacks has become a flood, from Britain, U.S.A. and many other countries. When the British catalogue of *Paperbacks in Print* was first issued in May 1960 it recorded 5,886 titles "in print and on sale" in Britain, a good many being American. The issue of June 1963 records 12,024 titles. They are classified under fifty-three subject headings, from Aeronautics and Anthropology to Veterinary Science and Wireless. Only a third of them are fiction.

Most paperbacks are reprints of books which were first published successfully in hard covers, but Sir Allen Lane began, before the war, to commission new books for first publication as Penguins, and other publishers have increasingly followed suit. Some important works of scholarship and science for the general reader have made their first appearance in paperback form, and a number of these have reversed the usual process by being reprinted later in hard covers.

The most important development since the war is the vast increase in the numbers of titles and in the sales. Next most important is the increase in serious works, which now include some hundreds of university textbooks. The range of sizes and prices has extended too. While the majority of paperbacks keep to the original Penguin size and sell at 2s. 6d. or 3s. 6d., some are much larger, often to make room for pictures or diagrams, and many are issued at higher prices, ranging from 5s. to 35s.

It is a common fallacy that popular paperbacks are cheap because they have paper covers. The cost of hard covers is only a small part of the total cost of a book. The most important factor in deciding the price is the number which can be printed at one time, that is, the number likely to be sold in a fairly short period. Some of the heaviest production costs—setting up the type, making blocks for illustrations if there are any, and getting the machine ready to print—are the same no matter how many copies are printed. If these costs are divided amongst a small number of copies only, the cost per copy is very high; but if a large number of copies is printed the cost per copy is much less. This is why most paperbacks are reprints of hard-cover editions which have already shown that they are popular books almost certain to have large sales in cheap editions. No one can be certain that an entirely new paperback will have a large sale, so the price must be high or the risk will be great. Many books never appear in cheap editions because their public is so small that they would sell no more copies at 5s. than at 50s., and so the publisher would suffer a heavy loss. There is one other important factor which helps to make paperbacks cheap; they are often printed on very cheap paper, which would not be good enough for more expensive books.

Why are paperbacks so popular? They have caught the taste and matched the spirit of the age. They are cheap; everyone feels that he can afford them. They are often bargains, and everyone loves a bargain. They have eye-catching covers and are displayed prominently on many bookstalls and in other places besides bookshops, so they reach the many people who (unhappily for themselves) never go into bookshops. They are light to carry, they go conveniently into pocket or handbag, and they take very little space on the bookshelf. Above all they are often very good books, which have already proved themselves in hard-cover editions.

It seems possible that they will change us from a nation of book-borrowers into a nation of book-owners, and that would be a boon indeed, for one gets far more enjoyment and satisfaction from books when one has chosen them as friends to remain permanently on one's own shelves. Borrowing only is never enough.

How Books can Help You

At the time of writing there are about 200,000 books in print in Britain, and over 26,000 new books and new editions are issued every year. A thousand newspapers and six thousand other periodicals are published. In addition very large numbers of books and periodicals in English and in many other languages are imported. Readers can obtain any publication which they need from any other country if they order it from a competent bookseller; there is in Britain none of the political censorship which prevents readers in some countries from obtaining many British publications. Furthermore, our publications, of all kinds, are among the cheapest in the world.

All this offers great opportunities. Whatever you may want to do, there is a book, and very often a periodical as well, which will help you to do it better, more easily and more enjoyably, whether it is making a model aeroplane, collecting postage stamps, learning to cook or to swim under water, growing roses or tomatoes, working for an examination in any subject, choosing a career and making progress in it, or learning for the pleasure of learning: in any of these or a thousand other things books and periodicals can be your best friends and helpers. And this is not all. There is a vast amount of good general reading for all moods and tastes, from the most amusing of light entertainment to the masterpieces of literature in poetry and prose. Through books we can learn from the greatest men of all times and all countries. A wealth of wisdom, knowledge and poetry is stored up in every bookshop and library.

So everyone can feel confident that the publications he or she needs do exist. The practical problem is to find out what they are and how to get hold of them.

Perhaps you want a book on astronomy, for example, and you do not know what books there are on the subject, and which are the best. One way of finding out is to go to your local public library. If it is a library of any size you will find there a collection of books on all subjects and a catalogue, which acts as a kind of index to the books on the shelves. You can search for Astronomy (or whatever subject interests you) in the catalogue, which in most libraries is arranged in alphabetical order. It will tell you what books the library has on the subject, and where to look for them. Then you can browse through the books on the shelves to see which appeal most to you. Of course, if it is a small library you may not find exactly what you need, and then it is a good idea to ask the librarian to advise you. Besides knowing the books in his own library the librarian has many reference books which tell him which are the best books on any subject you can think of, so he can easily find out which will help you. For example, he may turn to the back of any books which he has on your subject to see if the author has provided a list of books for further reading. (A great many books, including this one, have a list of this kind.) He may also look up your subject in encyclopaedias, for many encyclopaedias, especially the larger ones, give a list of relevant books at the end of almost every article.

Another pleasant way of finding out is by browsing in a bookshop. A good bookseller knows a great deal about books. He, too, has reference books to help him, he makes it his business to keep well informed of new books as they appear, and he can tell you what books you can buy on any subject. Some booksellers have complete lists of books published in cheap series: the World's Classics, Everyman's Library, Collins Classics, Nelson Classics and others. These lists are particularly useful if you want to read the best of the world's literature, the classics of fiction and drama, poetry, biography, travel and so on. If, on the other hand, you want to read contemporary literature and books of topical interest, you will find that many of the best are reprinted as cheap paperbacks. Booksellers can usually give lists of these as well, telling you what books are available as paperbacks.

You can read about the new books that are being published all the time in the book reviews in your daily newspaper and in weekly papers such as the *Observer*, the *Sunday Times*, the *Listener* or *Punch*. Then, too, there are periodicals, weekly or monthly, on special subjects such as stamp collecting or ponies, and these periodicals review new books in their own special field, and often contain publishers' advertisements as well.

Very often you do not want to read a whole book on a subject, you just want to find out a certain fact: what a word means; where Samarkand is; what coelo-canths or the Zimbabwe ruins are; who the Argonauts were; which is the largest city in the world. . . . One is always coming across questions of this kind, and there are books to answer them. Everyone knows that to find the spelling or the meaning of a word you look it up in a dictionary, and when you want to find a place you look it up in an atlas. Encyclopaedias, however, are the most useful reference books of all. The best encyclopaedias are storehouses of information of every kind and they can answer almost any question you can think of. A few dictionaries act as miniature encyclopaedias, for they include names of people and places as well as all the other words which are usually explained in dictionaries, and they have illustrations of all kinds of objects which show you what they are like much better than words alone could do. The most recent of these is the *Oxford Illustrated Dictionary*. If you want to know about famous people who are alive today, you can look them up in *Who's Who*, where you will find a brief account of their lives and achievements up to date. (A revised edition is published every year.) Yearbooks and almanacs contain a great deal of information about current events and the organisation of the world today. Perhaps the most useful of all is *Whitaker's Almanack*, which contains a summary of the events of the past year in all fields, literary and scientific as well as political; information about every country of the world; directories of anything from periodicals to public schools; lists of common abbreviations; astronomical events of the coming year; the members of Her Majesty's Government and the posts which they hold; and a great deal more assorted information besides.

Besides such general reference books as these there are others which give fuller information in a special field: dictionaries of literature and of the theatre, for example; encyclopaedias of music and of the religions of the world; "who's whos" of scientists and of authors; atlases of economics and politics. There are far too many to mention here, but you will soon find them when you browse in bookshops or libraries, and by using them you will gradually discover what sort of information to look for in each.

Nowadays, when human knowledge is extending so rapidly in all directions, it is more than ever important not only to have a growing store of information in one's head, but to know where to find out any of the thousand and one other things that one needs to know.

ACKNOWLEDGEMENTS AND BOOK LIST

The authors acknowledge gratefully their indebtedness to the following books.

Those recommended for school libraries are marked with an asterisk *. Any of these books may havo altered in price or gone out of print (o.p.) since this book was printed.

E.S.H.

J.H.

I. GENERAL

* *Chambers's encyclopedia.* 15 volumes. Newnes.

GLAISTER, GEOFFREY. *Glossary of the book.* Allen and Unwin, 1960. £6 6s.

* HARVEY, SIR PAUL. *The Oxford companion to English literature.* 3rd edition. Oxford University Press. 1946. 35s.

* *Oxford junior encyclopedia*, edited by Laura E. Salt and Robert Sinclair. Volume 4: Communications. Oxford University Press. 1951. 35s.

II. THE PAST

ALLEGRO, JOHN M. *The Dead Sea scrolls.* Penguin, 1956. 3s. 6d. (paperback).

BINNS, N. E. *Introduction to historical bibliography.* 2nd edition. Association of Assistant Librarians, 1962. 40s.

BLAND, DAVID. *A history of book illustration.* Faber, 1958. £4 4s.

* BLAND, DAVID. *The illustration of books.* 3rd edition. Faber, 1962. 30s.

BÜHLER, CURT F. *The fifteenth-century book.* Philadelphia, University of Pennsylvania Press, 1960.

* CARY, M., and HAARHOFF, T. J. *Life and thought in the Greek and Roman world.* Methuen, 1940. 12s. 6d. (paperback).

* COULTON, G. C. *Medieval panorama.* Cambridge University Press, 1938. o.p. Collins, 2 volumes, 9s. 6d. each (paperback).

COWELL, F. R. *Everyday life in ancient Rome.* Batsford, 1961. 18s.

CROSS, F. L. *The Oxford dictionary of the Christian Church.* Oxford University Press, 1957. £4.

DIRINGER, DAVID. *The alphabet, a key to the history of mankind.* Hutchinson, 1947. o.p.

DIRINGER, DAVID. *The illuminated book.* Faber, 1958. £6 6s.

* DIRINGER, DAVID. *Writing.* Thames and Hudson, 1962. 30s.

GARDINER, SIR ALAN. *Egypt of the Pharaohs.* Oxford University Press, 1961. 35s.

* HARVEY, SIR PAUL. *The Oxford companion to classical literature.* Corrected edition. Oxford University Press, 1951. 18s.

JOHNSON, A. F. *Type designs, their history and development.* 2nd edition. Grafton, 1959. 21s.

KENYON, SIR FREDERIC G. *Books and readers in ancient Greece and Rome.* 2nd edition. Oxford University Press, 1951. o. p.

MCKERROW, R. B. *An introduction to bibliography for literature students.* Oxford University Press, 1927. 28s.

MCLEAN, RUARI. *Modern book design.* Faber, 1958. 21s.

* MCMURTRIE, DOUGLAS C. *The book.* 3rd edition. Oxford University Press, 1943. 87s. 6d.

MUMBY, FRANK. *Publishing and bookselling, a history from the earliest times to the present day.* Revised edition, Cape, 1956. 42s.

* MURRAY, MARGARET A. *The splendour that was Egypt, a general survey of Egyptian culture and civilisation.* Sedgwick and Jackson, 1949. 35s.

* PIGGOTT, STUART (editor). *The dawn of civilisation.* Thames and Hudson, 1961. £8 8s.

PLANT, MARJORIE. *The English book trade: an economic history of the making and sale of books.* Allen and Unwin, 1939. o.p.

* RAYNER, JOHN. *Wood engravings by Thomas Bewick.* Penguin (King Penguin), 1947. 3s. 6d.

STEINBERG, S. H. *Five hundred years of printing.* Revised edition. Penguin, 1962. 8s. 6d. (paperback).

III. THE PRESENT

* CURWEN, HAROLD. *Printing.* Penguin (Puffin Picture Book), 1955. 3s. 6d. (paperback).

HAMPDEN, JOHN (editor). *The book world to-day.* Allen and Unwin, 1957. 21s.

HARRIS, RALPH, and HERBERT, A. P. *Libraries—free for all?* The Institute of Economic Affairs, 1962. 6s.

* JENNETT, SEÁN. *The making of books.* 2nd edition. Faber, 1956. 52s.

MCCOLVIN, LIONEL. *The chance to read, public libraries in the world to-day.* Phoenix House, 1956. o.p.

* MCCOLVIN, LIONEL. *How to find out.* Cambridge University Press, for the National Book League, 1947. o.p.

MUNFORD, W. A. *Penny rate: aspects of British public library history 1850–1950.* The Library Association, 1951. o.p.

* PENGUIN BOOKS. *Penguin progress.* Penguin, 1960. 2s. 6d. (paperback).

STRONG, L. A. G. *The writer's trade.* Methuen, 1953. o.p.

* TARR, JOHN C. *Printing to-day.* 3rd edition. Oxford University Press, 1949. o.p.

* TREASE, GEOFFREY. *The young writer.* Nelson, 1961. 7s. 6d.

UNWIN, SIR STANLEY. *The truth about publishing.* 7th edition. Allen and Unwin, 1960. 15s.

WILLIAMSON, HUGH. *Methods of book design.* Oxford University Press, 1956. 45s.

INDEX

References to illustrations are in **bold** type

advertising, 78
Alexandria, 18–19
alphabetic writing, 8, 16–17; **17**
Arabs, 33
Areopagitica, 42
Ashur-bani-pal, 11, 18
Asinius, Pollio, 21
Asser-bani-pal, 11, 18
atlas, 90
Atticus, Titus Pomponius, 20–21
Attikians, 21
Augustus, 21, 22
authors, 53ff., 63

Babylon, 10, 11
Baskerville, John, 44
bestiaries, 29
Bewick, Thomas, 44; **44**
Bible, 18, 24, 36
Biblia Pauperum, 31; **31**
binding, 25, 40, 47, 64, 71–72
black letter, 39, 42
block printing, 24–25, 31; **31**
blocking, 64, 71
Bodleian Library, 85
Bodoni, Giambattista, 44; **43**
bold type, 61
book clubs, 49
book design, 50–52, 59ff.
Book of Hours, 28
Book of Kells, 28
Book of the Dead, 15–16; **16**
bookselling, 62, 77, 80–82; Egypt, 15; Greece, 18; Rome, 21
bookshop, 89
British Council, 80, 85
British Museum, 10, 12, 14, 29, 85, 86
Byblos, 18

Cambridge University Library, 85
Canterbury Tales, 29, 37
casing, 47, 71–72
Caxton, William, 37; **38, 78**

censorship, 21, 42
Central Office of Information, 80
chained books, 28
Champollion, 14
Chinese, 8, 24–25, 31, 33, 34
clay tablets, 8–11, 17; **10, 11**
codex, 22; **23**
contract, 56, 59
copy, 64
copyright, 54
cuneiform, 10, 17; **11, 18**
cylinder press, 68; **69**

Dead Sea Scrolls, 22–24
demotic script, 14
Diamond Sutra, 24; **25**
Dictes or Sayengis of the Philosophers, 37
dictionary, 90
display type, 61
Dürer, Albrecht, 44
dust-jacket, 47, 63

Egypt, 7, 10, 11–16, 18
Elementary Education Act (1870), 48
encyclopaedia, 89, 90
Eumenes, 19
Everyman's Library, 52, 89

flong, 68
forme, 67; **68**
Fourdrinier papermaking machine, 45, 64; **65**

galley, 66–67; **66**
Gilgamesh, Epic of, 11
gothic type, 39, 42–43, 50
Greeks, 8, 11, 14, 17–18
Gutenberg, John, 35, 36

half-tone, 73–74; **73, 74**
Harris Papyrus, 12
herbals, 29
hieratic script, 14
hieroglyphics, 10, 13–14; **13**

Holbein, Hans, 44

ideographs, 8, 17
Iliad, 11, 18
illuminated manuscripts, 26–29
illustration, 41, 44–45, 48, 52, 63, 70, 72ff.:
  half-tone, 73–74; **73**: line block, 72–73:
  lithography, 47, 60, 75–76; **74**: metal engraving, 44: photogravure, 60, 74–75; **74**:
  wood engraving, 44, 72: woodcut, 31, 41, 45
incunabula, 39
index, 64
Intertype, 46
italic, 39, 42, 61

Japanese, 8, 24
justification, 65

Kelmscott Press, 50
König, Friedrich, 46
Korea, 25

Lane, Sir Allen, 52, 86–87
Lanston, Tolbert, 46
Layard, Sir Austen Henry, 11
layout, 62
libraries, 41, 48, 82–86, 89; Alexandria, 18;
  Assyria, 11; Constantinople, 22; Pergamon,
  19; Rome, 20–21
Lindisfarne Gospels, 27–28; **27**
line block, 72–73
Linear B, 9
Linotype, 46, 52
literary agents, 54
literary critics, 58
lithography, 47, 60, 75–76; **74**
Lucian, 21

make-ready, 67
Manutius, Aldus, 39, 60; **39, 40**
Marco Polo, 34
Martial, 21
matrix, 66
matrix case, 66; **66**
Mergenthaler, Otto, 46
Mesopotamia, 8, 10

metal engraving, 44
Milton, John, 42
miniatures, 29
Monotype, 46, 52, 64; **65**
Morris, William, 50; **51**
Morte d'Arthur, 37

National Library of Scotland, 85
National Library of Wales, 85
newspapers, 42, 48, 53, 69, 90
Nile, 10, 11

paper, 31–34, 45, 64; **33**
paperbacks, 49, 60, 71, 86–88
Paperbacks in Print, 86
papyrus, 11–15, 17–20, 22, 26; **12, 20**
parchment, 18, 19–20, 22, 28, 31, 34
patronage, 42
Penguin Books, 52, 86–87
Pergamon, 19
periodicals, 90
Persians, 8
Phoenicians, 16–17, 18
photogravure, 60, 74–75; **74**
photosetting, 47
pictographs, 7–8, 10, 13; **8, 10**
Pi-Sheng, 25
prelims, 62
printing, China, 24–25; Japan, 24; Korea, 25
printing, invention of, 34–41
printing press, 35, 41, 45–46, 67–69; **36**
private presses, 50–52
proofs, 62–63, 67
Ptolemy, 18
publishers' devices, **58–59**
publishers' readers, 58
publishing, 54ff.; Rome, 20–21

Queen Mary's Psalter, 29

reprint publishing, 49
reviews, 77
roman alphabet, 8
roman type, 39, 42–44
Romans, 20
romances, 29

Rosetta Stone, 14
rotary press, 69
royalties, 56
rubrics, 14, 26
Recuyell of the Histories of Troye, 37

sales, 79–80
scriptorium, 26
scroll, 20, 23; **20, 23**: Egyptian, 11–13; Greek,
    18; Roman, 20
Senefelder, Aloysius, 47
Sheridan, R. B., 53
signature, 69–70; **70**
Society of Authors, 56
specimen pages, 62
Stanhope, Earl, 45
stereo, 68–69; **69**
Sumerians, 8, 10, 11

syllabic writing, 8

three-decker novel, 48
Times, The, 45, 46, 60
title page, 41, 62
Trinity College, Dublin, 85
type, movable, 25, 34ff.
typeface, 60
typesetting, 46

vellum, 19, 22

Walker, Sir Emery, 50
wax tablets, 20; **20**
Whitaker's Almanack, 90
Who's Who, 76, 90
wood engraving, 44, 72
woodcut, 31, 41, 45